CW01649238

Van Gogh and the sunflowers

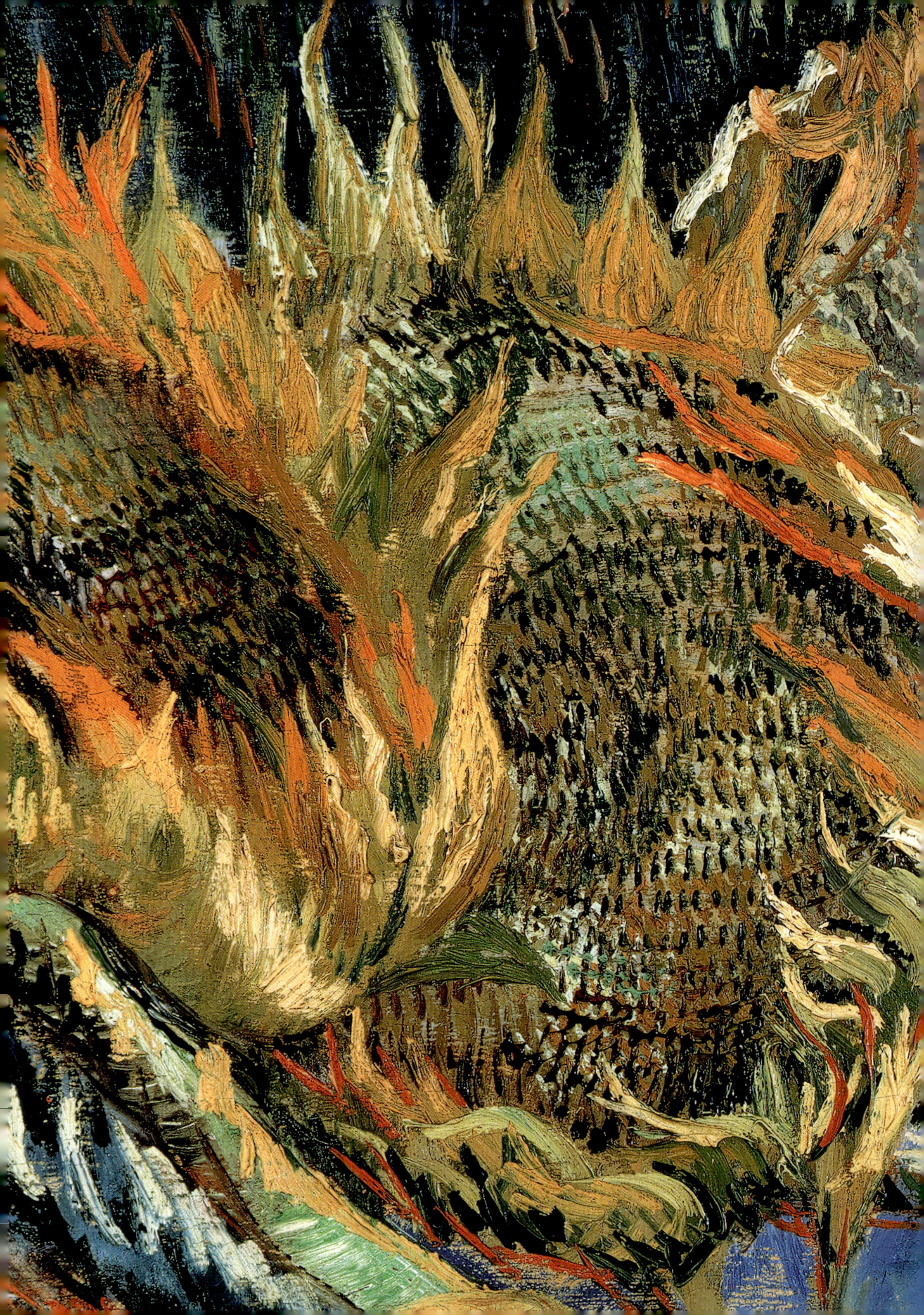

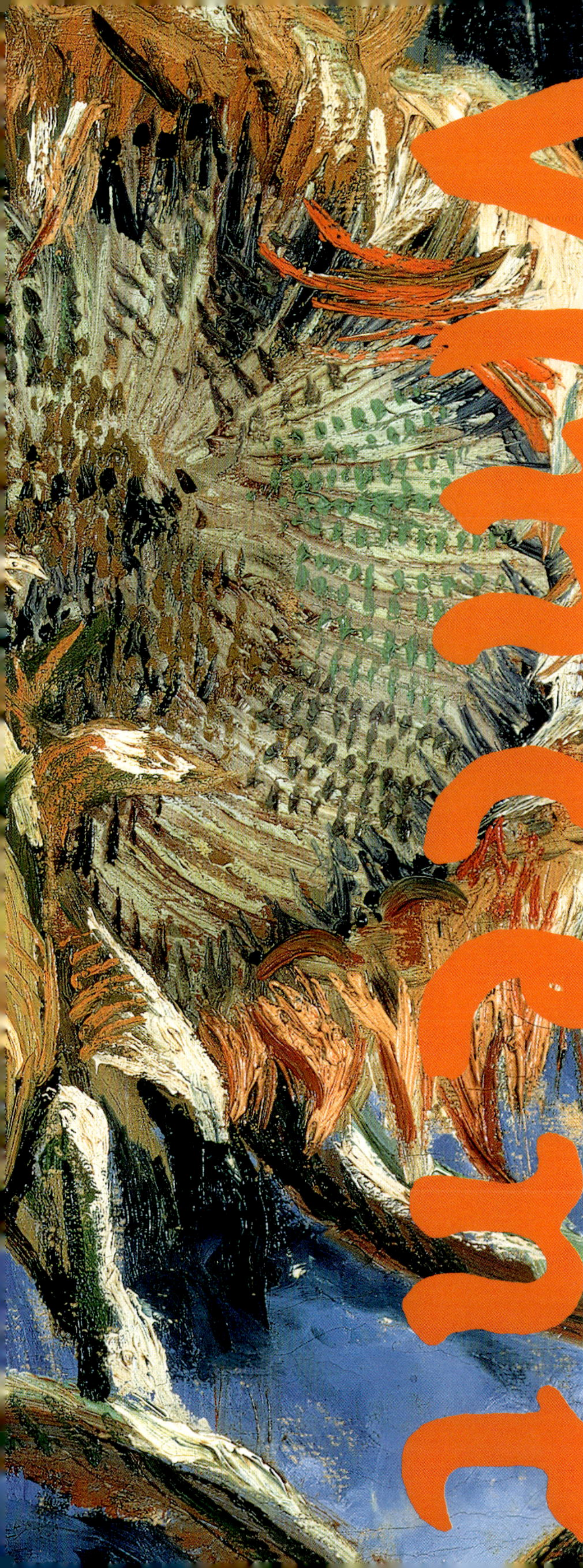

VAN GOGH
and the sunflowers

Louis van Tilborgh

VAN GOGH MUSEUM

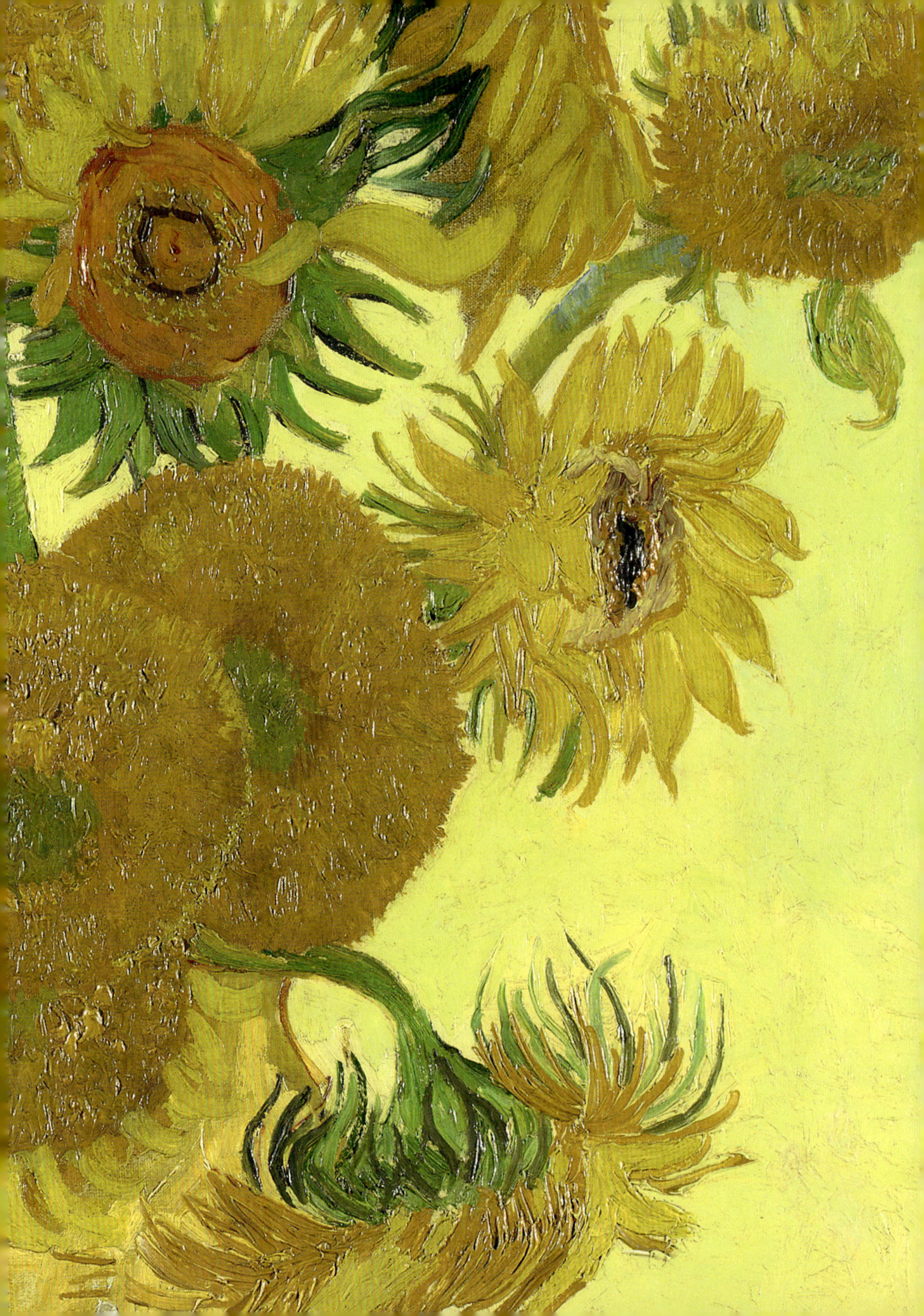

GREAT ARTISTS often live on in our memory because of a single work of art that seems to encapsulate their artistic qualities. With Leonardo da Vinci it is the *Mona Lisa*, with Rembrandt *The Night Watch*, with Seurat *La Grande Jatte* and with Van Gogh *Sunflowers*. It is said that in this still life Van Gogh surpassed himself as an artist, and as a result it is now regarded as his *chef d'oeuvre*. As it happens, he painted not one work with sunflowers but eleven, but when one reads '*Sunflowers*' one immediately thinks of the painting now in The National Gallery in London (37). This still life from the Arles period meant a great deal to Van Gogh, and at the end of 1888 and beginning of 1889 he made two more versions of it, which are now in the Seiji Togo Memorial Sompo Japan Museum of Art in Tokyo and the Van Gogh Museum in Amsterdam (46, 49). The subject is a Provençal vase with sixteen sunflowers, some of which have gone to seed. Although Van Gogh also used green, blue and orange, it is yellow that predominates and charms us with its many shades. This painting has a remarkable significance that cannot be seen in isolation from Van Gogh's other still lifes with sunflowers. They will all be discussed in this book, but first it is worth taking a look at Van Gogh as a flower painter and discover why he became so engrossed in this particular genre.

1
Vincent van Gogh
Sunflowers, 1888
(detail fig. 37)
The National Gallery, London

LOVE OF NATURE

Van Gogh loved flowers his whole life long, and was as happy to see them in a vase as in a field or garden. In early 1882, when he had left his parents' home after a furious argument, he bought flowers and 'a couple of boxes of bulbs', probably daffodils and hyacinth or crocus bulbs, as we can conclude from his correspondence, for his new, sparsely furnished home in The Hague, despite the fact that he was very short of money. We also know that he put 'flowers in front of the window' when his lover Sien Hoornik returned from hospital after the birth of her son, and he was really moved when his parents surprised him with the gift of a bunch of flowers from their garden when he was living in Dordrecht in 1877.

Van Gogh grew up in the country village of Zundert in the province of Brabant, and it was this rural setting that gave him his 'great love of animals and plants', to quote his sister Elisabeth. He knew where he could find rare plants like the flowering rush, and learned that if there were dandelions in the meadows they would soon be followed by daisies and violets. His parents regarded this love of and knowledge about nature as part of a young person's general development, and encouraged it in all their children. Whenever there was an opportunity the family went out for an hour's walk each day, and when plants were in flower they picked 'a thing or two, enough to fill a flower basket'.

His mother, above all, had a deep love of nature, and when Van Gogh painted her portrait from memory in 1888 (2) he showed her and his sister Willemien against the background of a garden with dahlias of every hue, scarlet geraniums, and pale green and red cabbages. Like his mother, Van Gogh loved informal gardens like this, and sought them out wherever he was, and it is tempting to trace this passion back to his parents' garden in Zundert. We know from Elisabeth that it contained currant and raspberry bushes and flower-beds with bright red geraniums, mignonettes and moss roses, flowering plants closely related to purslane. The view was idyllic, consisting of a small stream with fields of rye beyond and, on the horizon, 'a light green band where the meadows lay, fertile fields'.

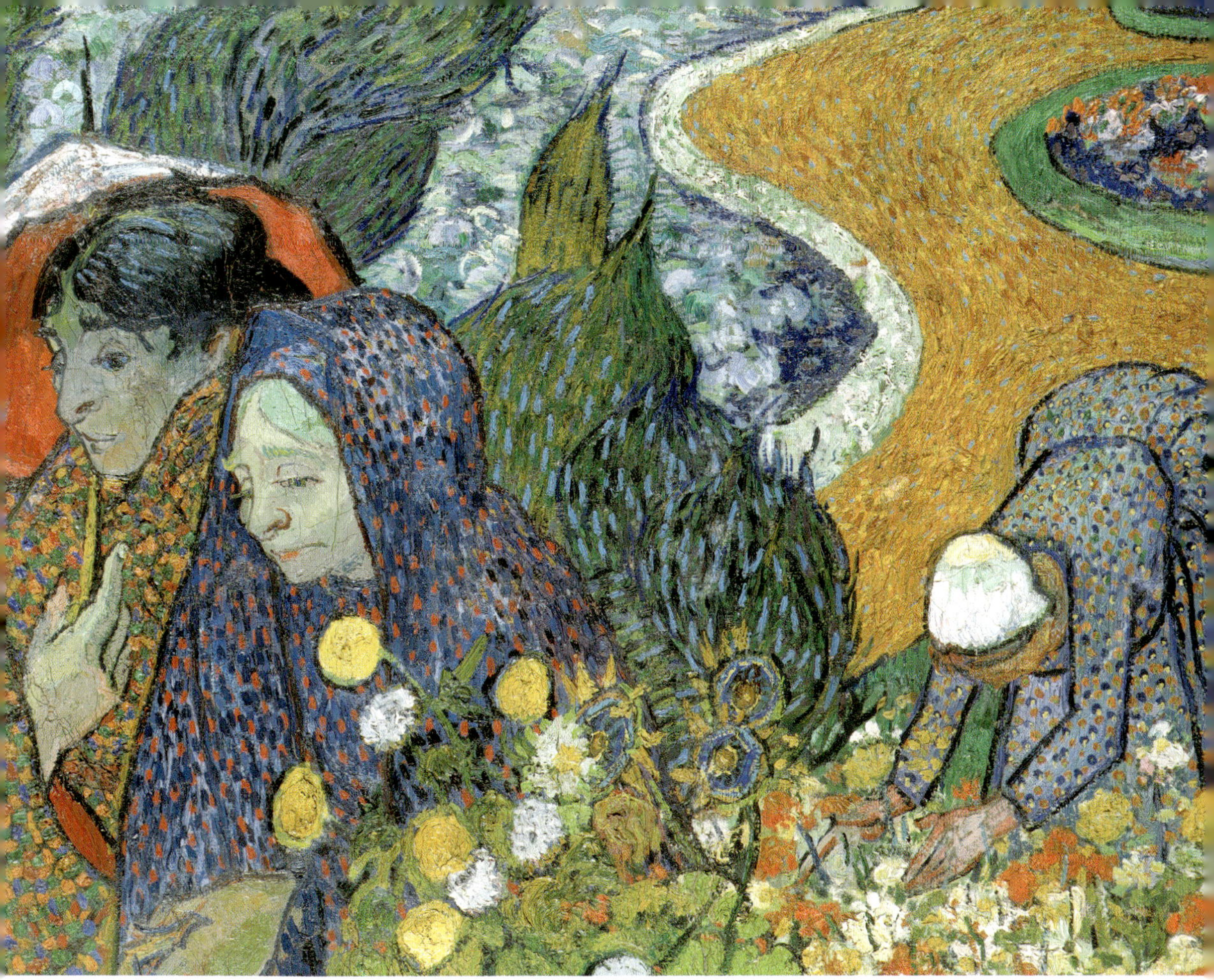

Van Gogh moved to the city at the age of sixteen, and from then on was filled with longing for this rural life. Whether he was living in The Hague, London or Paris, he was on the lookout for 'a glimpse of some bit of the country, never mind what'. The pain was eased by visiting the local parks and flower markets, because it was 'good to love flowers, and pine branches, and ivy, and hawthorn hedges', as he wrote in 1877. Later, when he was painting and drawing, he said that studying 'a blade of grass, the branch of a fir tree, an ear of wheat' brought him wisdom and calm. He explained to his sister Willemien in 1889, for 'If you want to do as the artists do, go and look at the red and white poppies with their bluish leaves, their buds soaring on gracefully bent stems. The hours of trouble and strife will know how to find us without our going to look for them'.

2
Vincent van Gogh
Reminiscence of the garden at Etten, 1888
The State Hermitage Museum, St Petersburg

FLOWER STILL LIFES

Despite his love of flowers, Van Gogh painted fewer of them than one might expect early in his career. They were sometimes included as details in his views of parks and gardens, but were never treated as a subject in their own right. He wanted to follow in the footsteps of artists like Jean-François Millet, Théodore Rousseau, Anton Mauve and Jozef Israëls, and these leading lights of the School of Barbizon and the Hague School painted landscapes or figures, of peasants and other people, but never still lifes of flowers. He followed their example, and one searches in vain for a mention of flower painters in the letters from his Dutch period. They lay outside his sphere of artistic interest.

That is not at all surprising, for still lifes had been at the bottom of the hierarchy of genres since time immemorial. Painting lifeless things could not appeal to the imagination, and the 'true', universal artist did better to avoid the genre altogether, unless he wanted to demonstrate his mastery of all subjects. Despite this poor reputation, there were many still-life painters active around the middle of the nineteenth century, and they 'gnawed like rats' at the traditional hierarchy, as the French critic Jules-Antoine Castagnary put it so vividly. Still-life painting obviously had important advantages over other genres. If you wanted to excel in figure painting you had to hire models, which was expensive, and if landscape was your ambition you were forced to leave the sanctuary of your warm, wind-proof studio. These drawbacks were pleasantly absent from still-life painting.

There was, too, quite a market for still lifes, and particularly for those of flowers. As a result, many artists specialized in them, and the financial rewards even tempted some painters of figure pieces or landscapes to the genre. Henri Fantin-Latour, for instance, who preferred allegorical, romantic subjects, painted many still lifes of flowers, especially at the beginning of his career, although they did leave him with a permanently guilty conscience. 'Since I can dispose of them I regard it as doing business. I feel like an art dealer. Never before have I had so many ideas about art in my head, and now I'm forced to paint flowers', he complained. 'When I'm painting them – standing in front of peonies and roses – I'm thinking of Michelangelo. It can't go on like this.'

Van Gogh was also eager to earn money, but initially he did not consider it a viable option to abandon his favourite subjects for still lifes of flowers. He had painted still lifes of objects in the winters of 1881–82 and 1884–85, but these he regarded merely as exercises in form and colour. It was only at the end of his time in Nuenen, when he understood that his brother Theo could not and would not support him financially whatever the cost, that he compromised. He was prepared, temporarily, to master good, popular subjects, and pinned his hopes on portraits, townscapes and still lifes of flowers.

3
Vincent van Gogh
Earthenware vase with flowers, 1885
Philadelphia Museum of Art

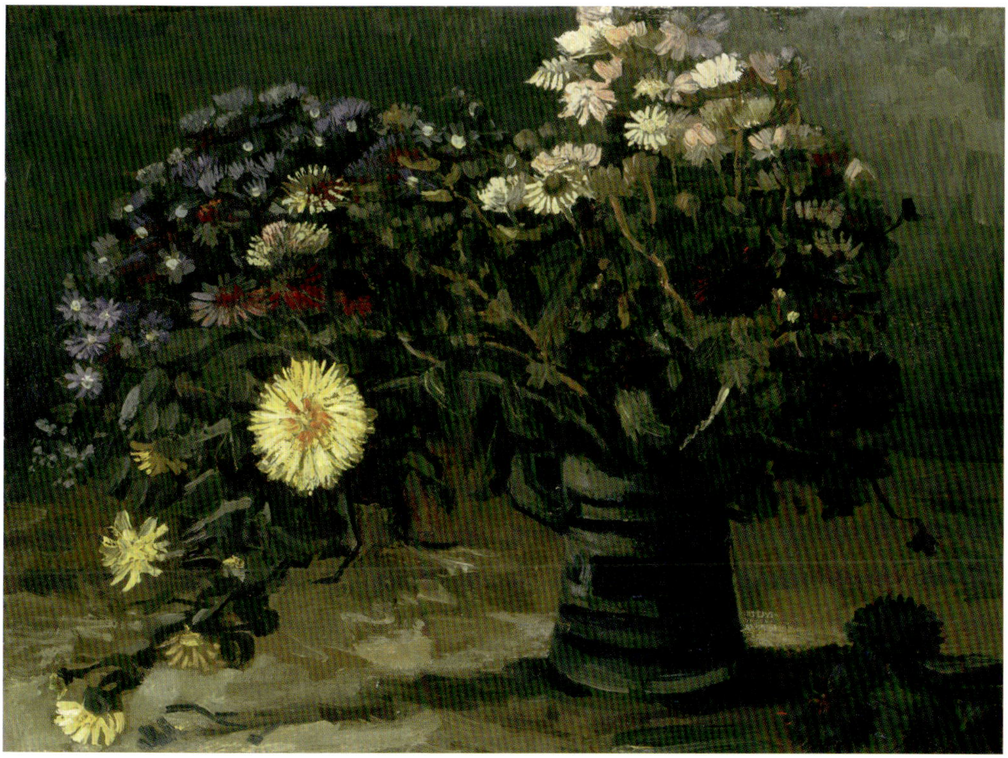

Although his first flower pieces date from this period (3), it was only in the following year, 1886, that he really began to immerse himself in the subject. He was living with Theo in Paris at the time, and throughout the summer he painted 'hardly anything but flowers', for which helpful friends sent him 'a beautiful delivery' each week, and thanks to the forty or so still lifes that survive we know what they gave him. They were flowers typical of the season – peonies, poppies and cornflowers in the early summer, and in the late summer hollyhocks, gladioli and Chinese asters. He had hoped to sell these still lifes, but when he failed to do so he carried on producing them 'in order to make his next paintings more colourful', as Theo wrote to their mother.

This expansion of Van Gogh's repertoire went hand in hand with a broadening of his taste. He now suddenly learned to appreciate the merits of artists like Ernest Quost and Georges Jeannin (4, 5), partly thanks to

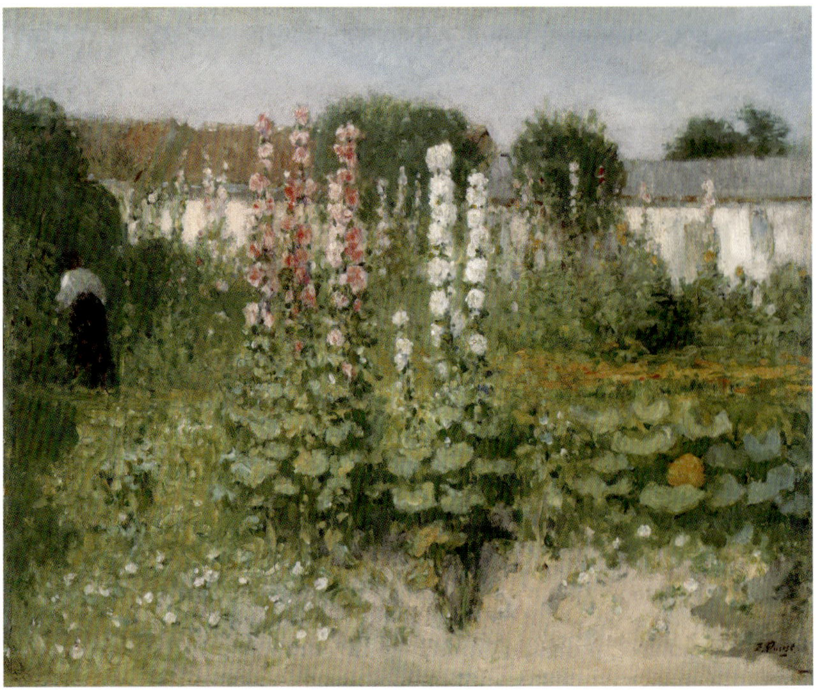

4
Ernest Quost
Field with hollyhocks,
c. 1880
Van Gogh Museum,
Amsterdam

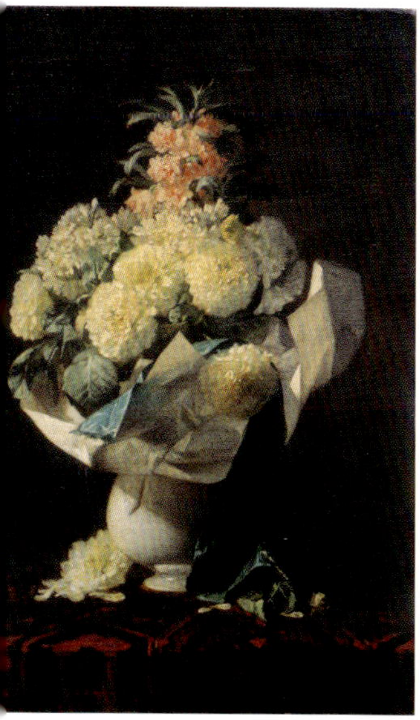

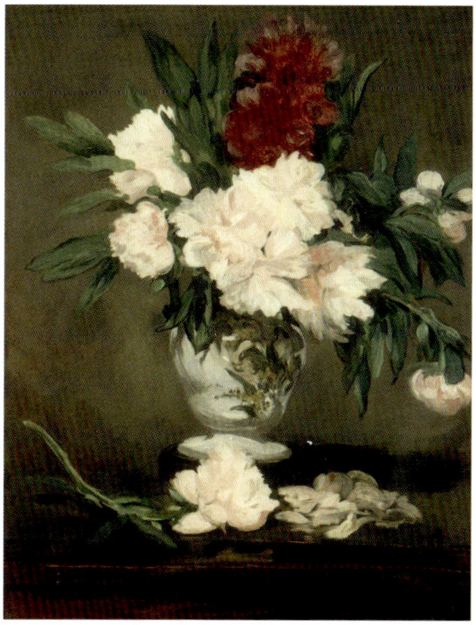

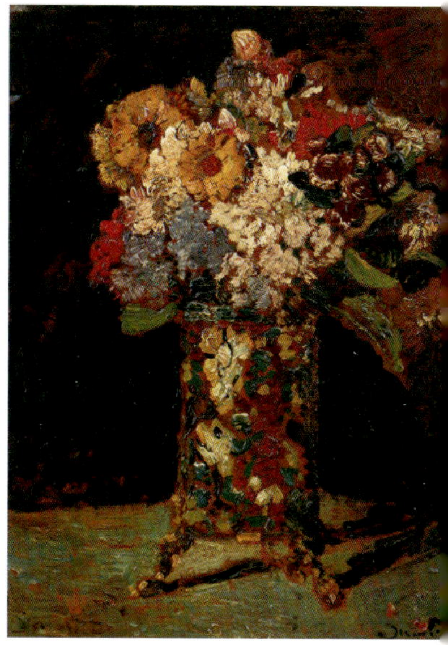

Theo, who was the manager of a branch of the Paris art dealers Boussod, Valadon et Cie and had sold several works by these flower painters. They cost around 250 francs each, and it can be assumed that Van Gogh, who was paid only 50 francs a painting, hoped to do business with his brother's circle of buyers. Theo owned two paintings by Jeannin (5), but nothing by Quost. It was a gap in his collection, and in 1890 Vincent was to suggest making an exchange of work with this Montmartre painter. He died shortly afterwards, however, whereupon Quost gave Theo a work as a present (4).

Vincent praised the feeling for nature that these two painters had, but from an artistic point of view he felt more attracted to Édouard Manet, a still life of whose he saw at an auction in June 1886 (6). It stood out for its airy, free manner, but in Vincent's view the peonies were nevertheless still instantly recognisable. 'As much in harmony and as much a *flower* as anything could be, and yet painted in a solid, thick impasto', he later wrote. 'That's what I'd call simplicity of technique.' He was also very moved by the still lifes of flowers by the Provençal artist Adolphe Monticelli. In the work of this colourist, who had died shortly before, he recognised his own

5
Georges Jeannin
Vase of flowers, c. 1875
Van Gogh Museum, Amsterdam

6
Édouard Manet
Peonies in a vase, 1864
Musée d'Orsay, Paris

7
Adolphe Monticelli
Still life of flowers, c. 1875
Van Gogh Museum, Amsterdam

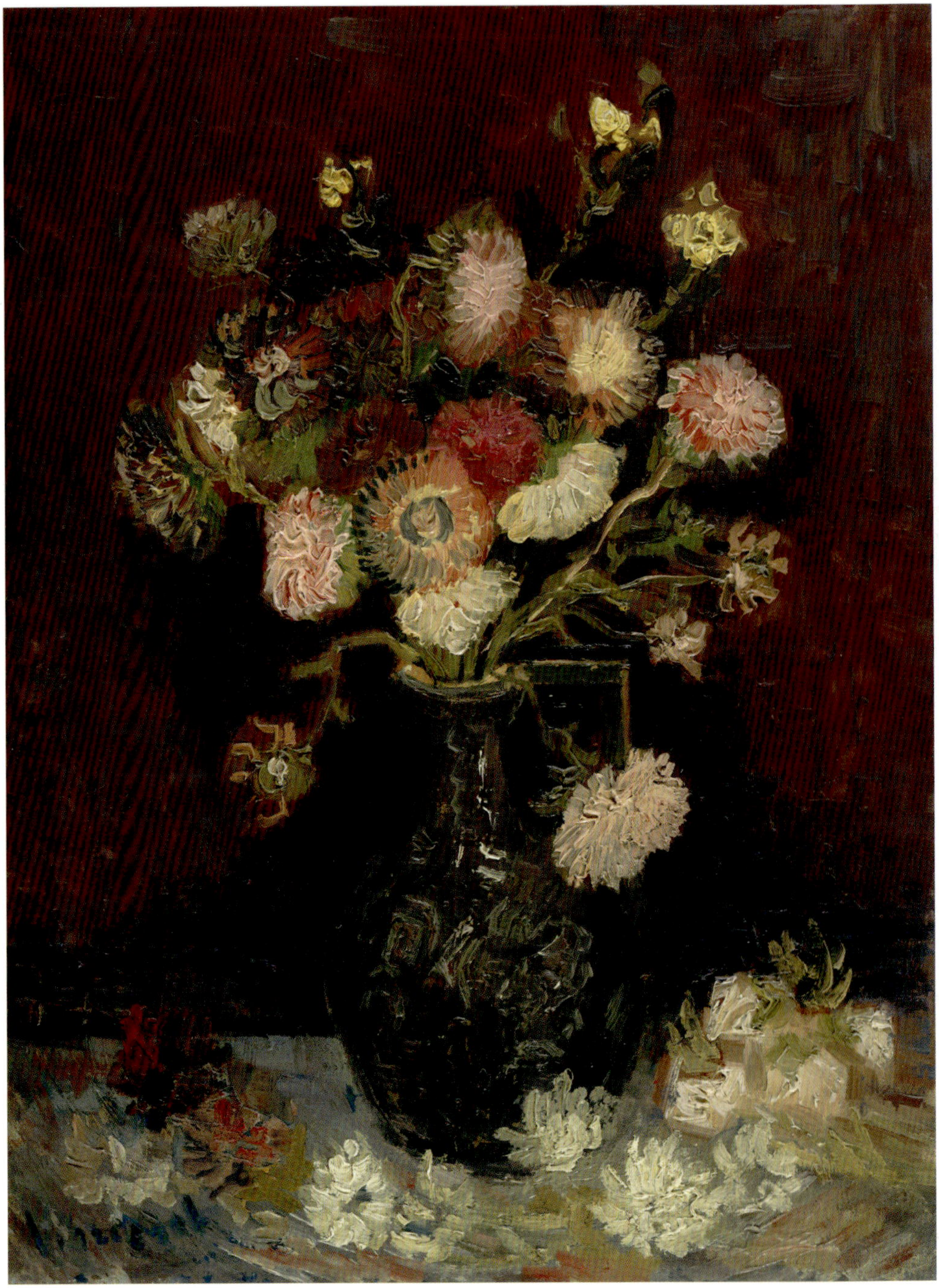

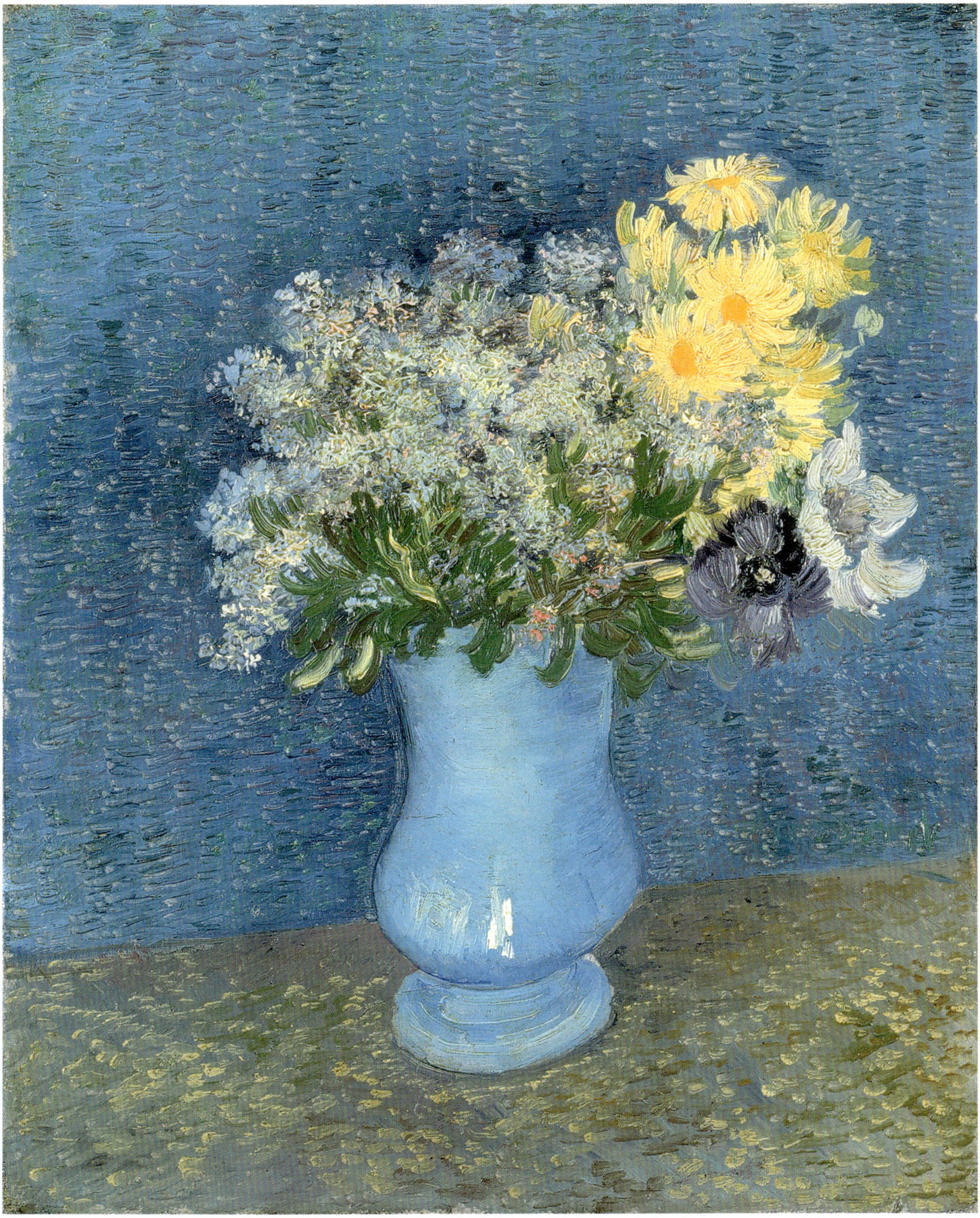

<8
Vincent van Gogh
Vase of Chinese asters and gladioli, 1886
Van Gogh Museum, Amsterdam

<9
Vincent van Gogh
Vase of lilacs, daisies and anemones, 1887
Musée d'art et d'histoire, Geneva

quest for bold, bright colours and an unpolished manner of painting. He admired Monticelli so much that he even managed to persuade Theo to buy one of his flower pieces (7). This work, which was 'a better piece of painting and more beautiful than a bouquet by Diaz', who was Monticelli's role model, showed, according to Vincent, that it was possible to gather 'together in a single panel the whole range of his richest and most perfectly balanced tones'. Unfortunately that richness is now masked by the highly yellowed layer of varnish, which has proved very difficult to remove.

Van Gogh opted for conventional, or at least not very experimental, compositions in an attempt to make his flower pieces more saleable. He always placed the vase right in the middle, and often resorted to depicting a few loose blooms in the foreground to enliven the picture – a device which had been popular since the 1830s. He sometimes included some faded flowers with broken stalks in the bouquet, which also helped to make the scene less stiff (8). Although he never sold any of these paintings, he did try to interest potential buyers. He had a small success in the early months of 1887, when he was allowed to hang most of his flower paintings in the Tambourin restaurant run by his lover Agostina Segatori.

In the spring Van Gogh again began painting flowers, possibly with the aim of adding new still lifes to his work in Le Tambourin (9), but these were in a rather different style. In the course of the winter he had finally broken with the old models from his Dutch period and had switched to the most modern movement in art. As a colourist, he built on the advances made by Impressionism and Neo-Impressionism, but in quite a free and personal way. This new exercise in the genre was limited to just a few paintings, but there was a revival at the height of summer, when he became fascinated by a single type – the sunflower.

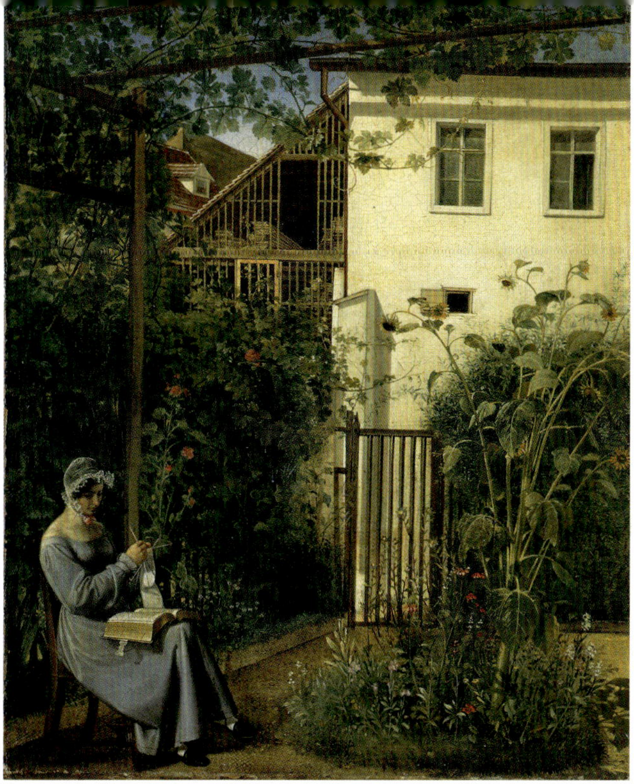

10
Erasmus von Engert
Viennese garden,
c. 1828–30
Alte Nationalgalerie, Staatliche Museen zu Berlin

SUNFLOWERS

Helianthus annuus, to give the sunflower its Latin name, is an exotic plant from America. In the sixteenth century Spanish seamen brought seeds of it back to Europe, where it became popular as a decorative plant. The annual flower could be seen in the gardens of the aristocracy, but its popularity waned towards the end of the eighteenth century. Many people regarded it as coarse, and it disappeared from ornamental gardens. Soon afterwards, though, around 1800, it was given a new lease of life in the less rigidly arranged gardens of the middle classes **(10)**. It had turned out that *Helianthus annuus* needed little care after it was sown, and that it flourished in any soil, provided there was sun. It then acquired a new reputation. This tall plant with its strong, rather hairy stem and bright yellow petals, formally known as ray flowers, was no longer regarded as exotic but as everyday and above all rustic. It became a standard in gardens of an informal, rural nature **(12)**, such as those of Claude Monet **(11)** and Gustave Caillebotte.

>11
Claude Monet
The artist's garden at Vétheuil, 1880
National Gallery of Art, Washington

>12
Édouard Manet
Washer woman (Le linge), 1875
The Barnes Foundation, Merion, PA

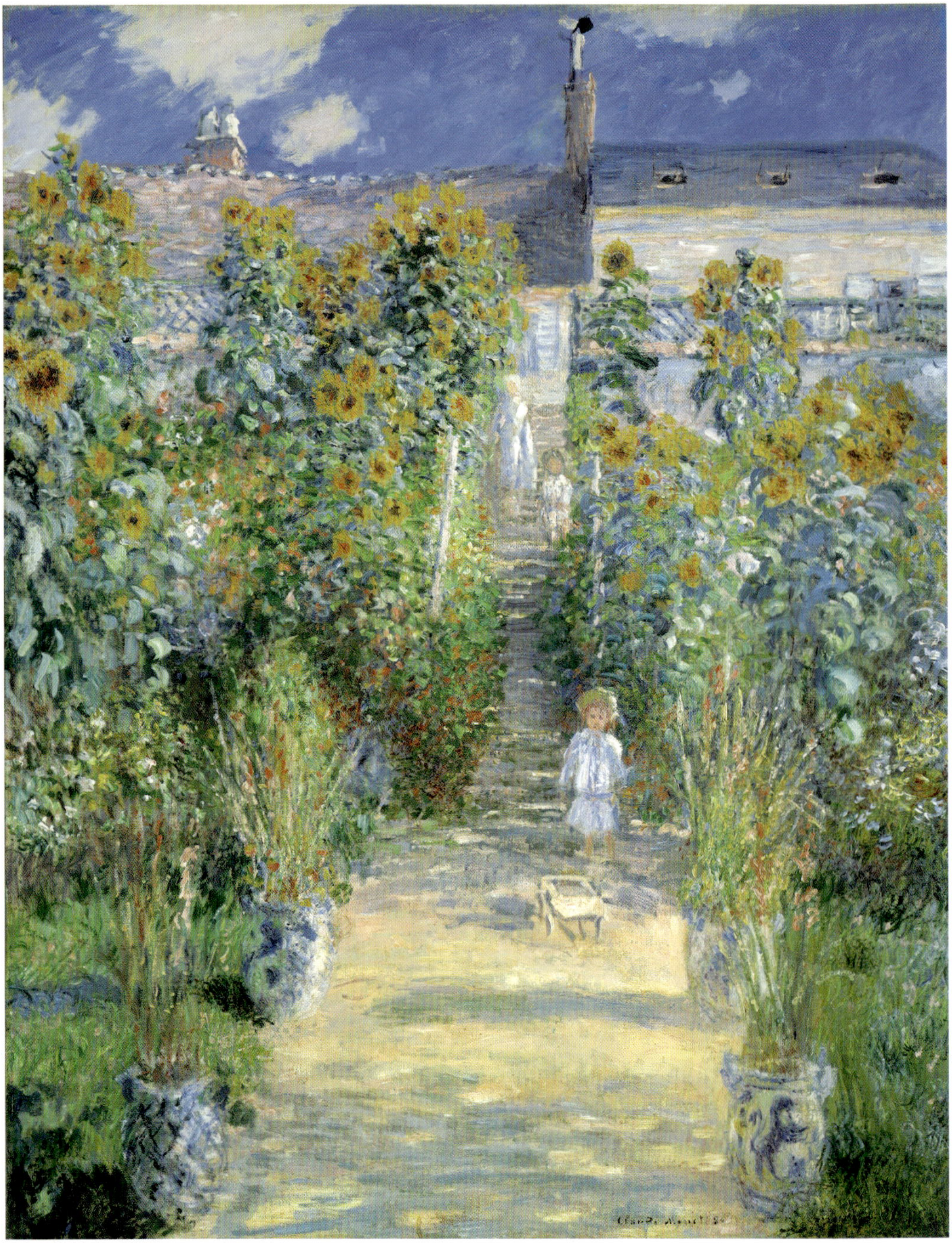

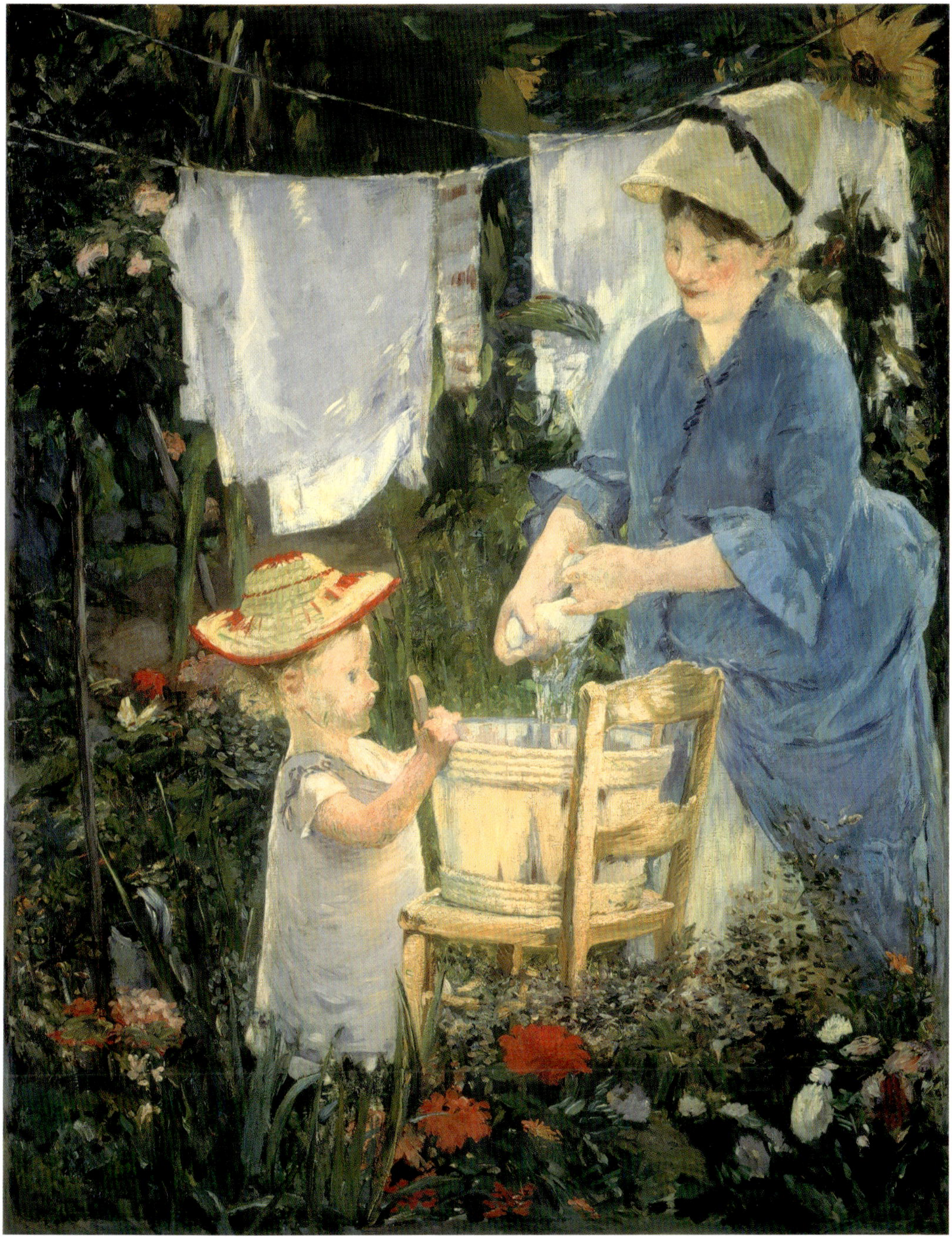

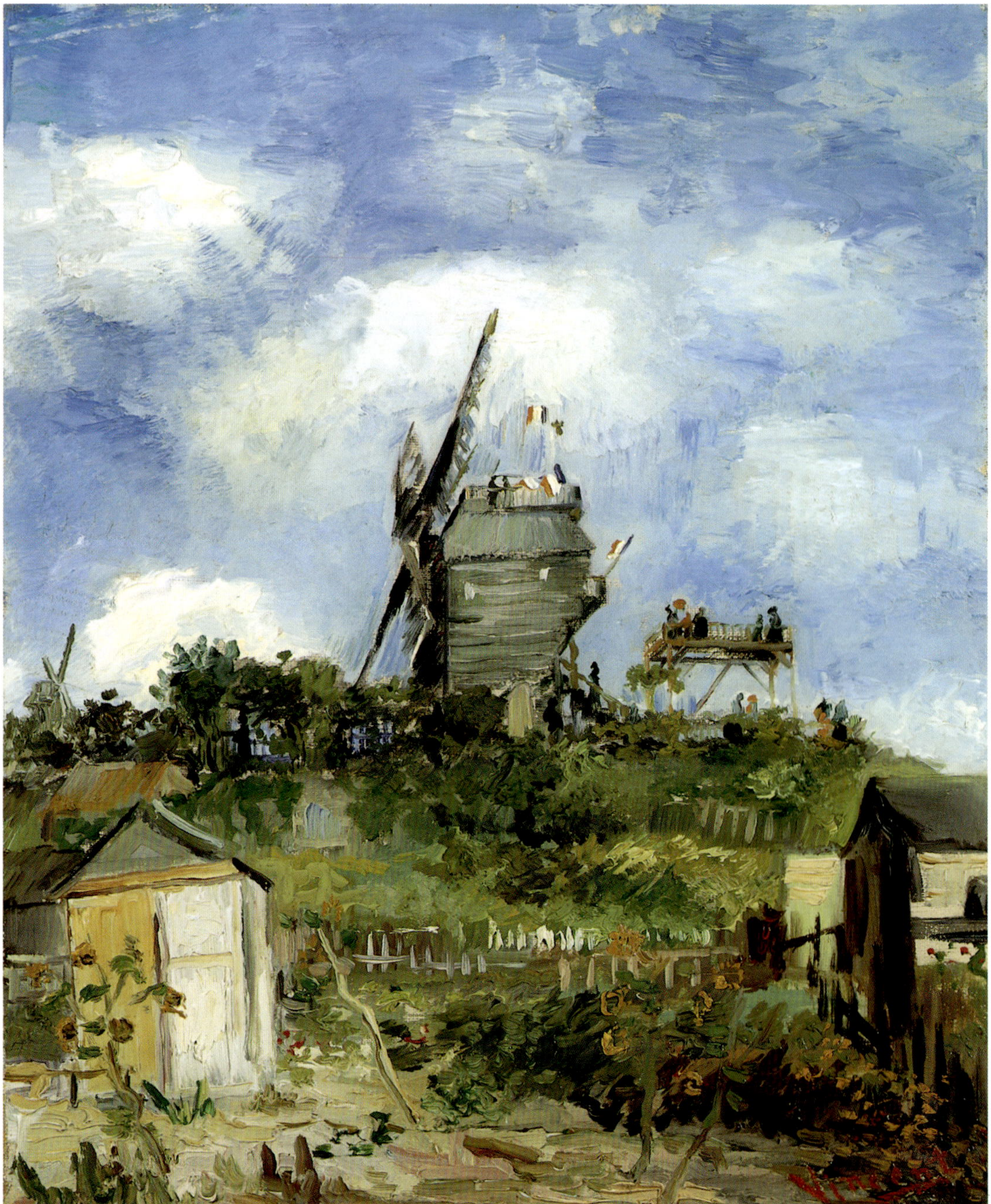
Vincent

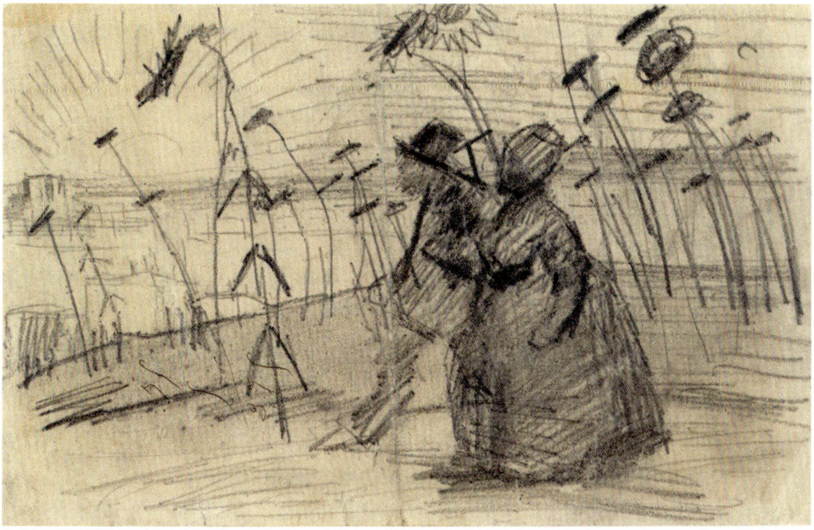

13
Vincent van Gogh
The Blute-Fin windmill, 1886
Kelvingrove Art Gallery and Museum, Glasgow

14
Vincent van Gogh
Strolling couple, 1887
Van Gogh Museum, Amsterdam

Van Gogh had shown an early interest in gardens of this kind with sunflowers as the eye-catching element. In 1883, when he was living in The Hague, he made a painting of a bleaching field with sunflowers which has unfortunately since been lost. When he went to live in Paris his interest was piqued by the rustic vegetable gardens on the hill of Montmartre, which were dotted with numerous tall sunflowers in the summer. He depicted them in 1886 in the foreground of his painting of the Blute-Fin windmill (13), but it was not until the following summer, when his longing for the countryside had grown acute, that he exploited the subject to the full (14–17). In one study he painstakingly recorded the appearance of one huge specimen at least two metres tall (16). At the end of the flowering season he also brought several large sunflowers that had gone to seed back to his studio, where he studied them in four exceptional still lifes (18–21).

The flower heads were too heavy for his usual vases, so he painted them lying on a surface against an indeterminate background, probably a table. Although born of necessity, this was not unusual as a composition. In addition to painting bouquets in vases there was a nineteenth-century vogue for showing flowers strewn seemingly haphazardly on the

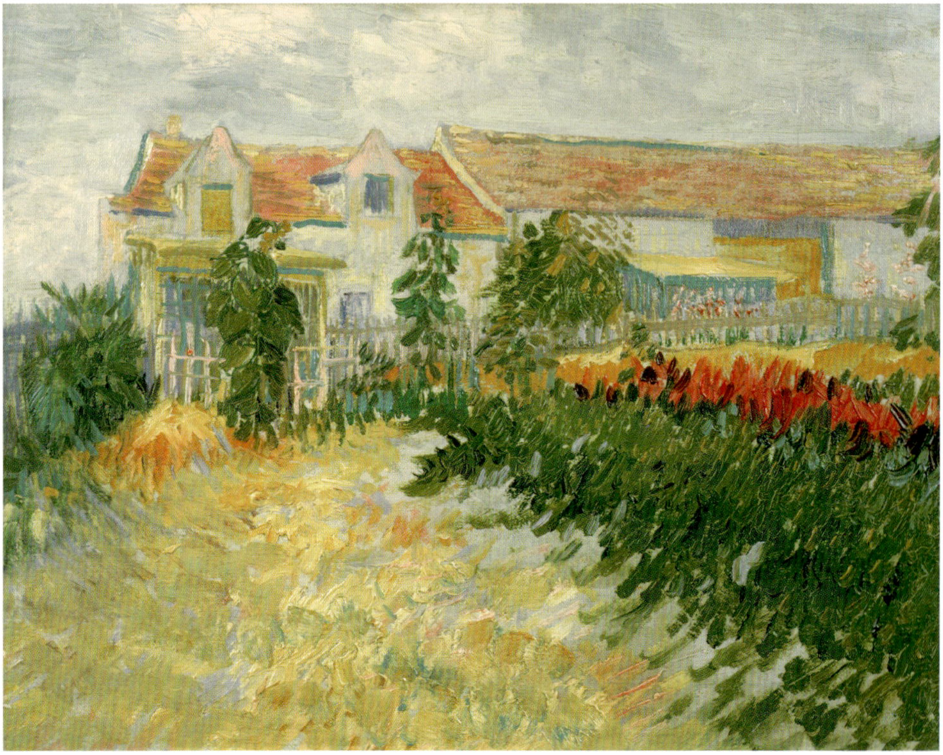

15
Vincent van Gogh
Sunflowers in Debray's garden near the Blute-Fin windmill, 1887
Private collection

16
Vincent van Gogh
Vegetable garden with sunflower, 1887
Van Gogh Museum, Amsterdam

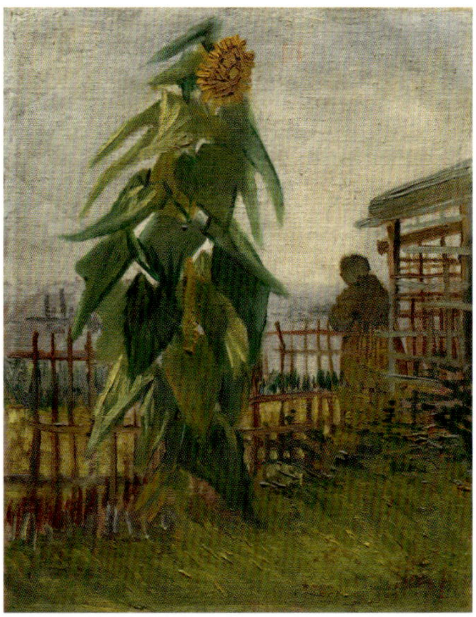

17
Vincent van Gogh
Shed with sunflowers, 1887
Van Gogh Museum, Amsterdam

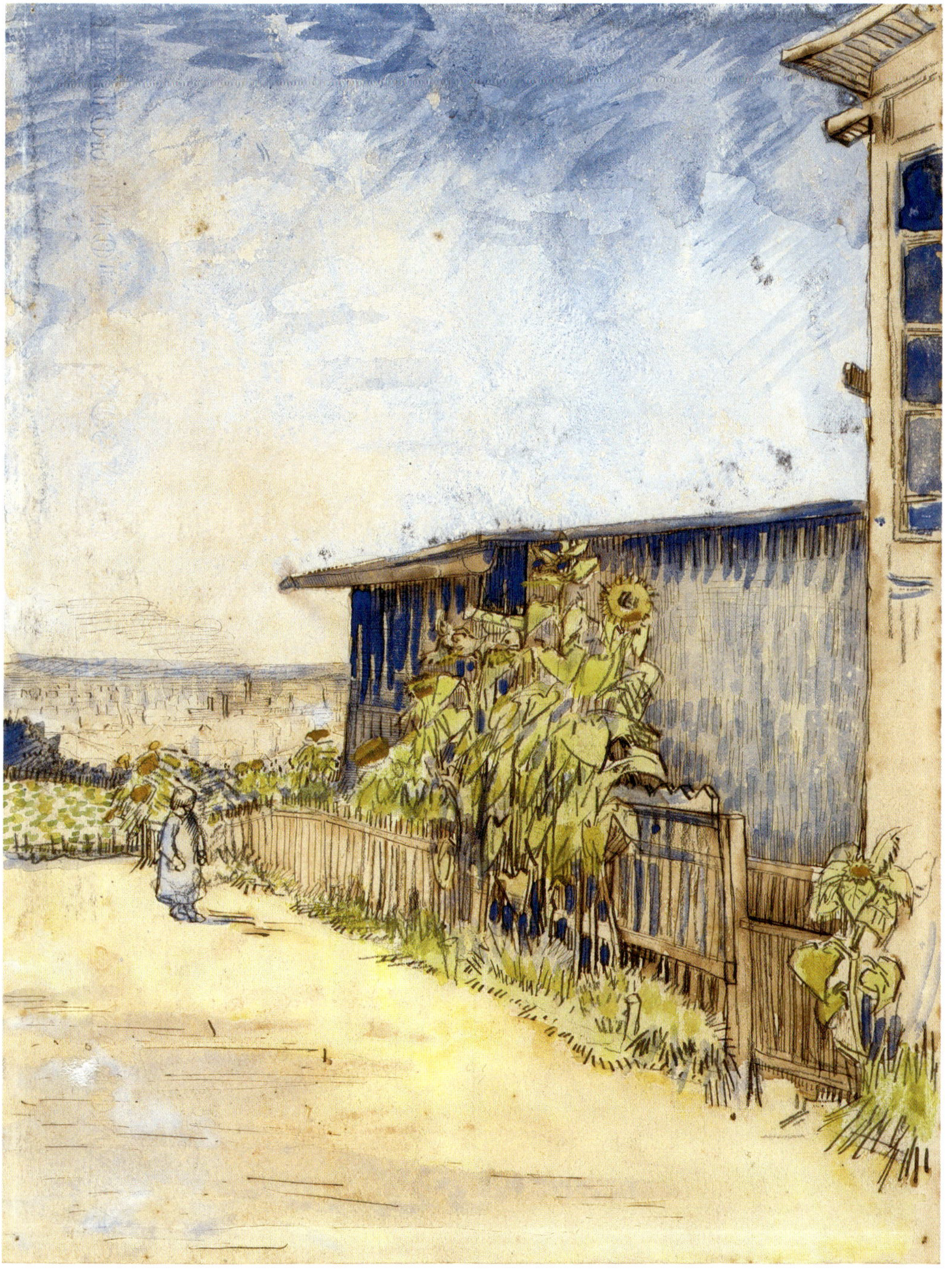

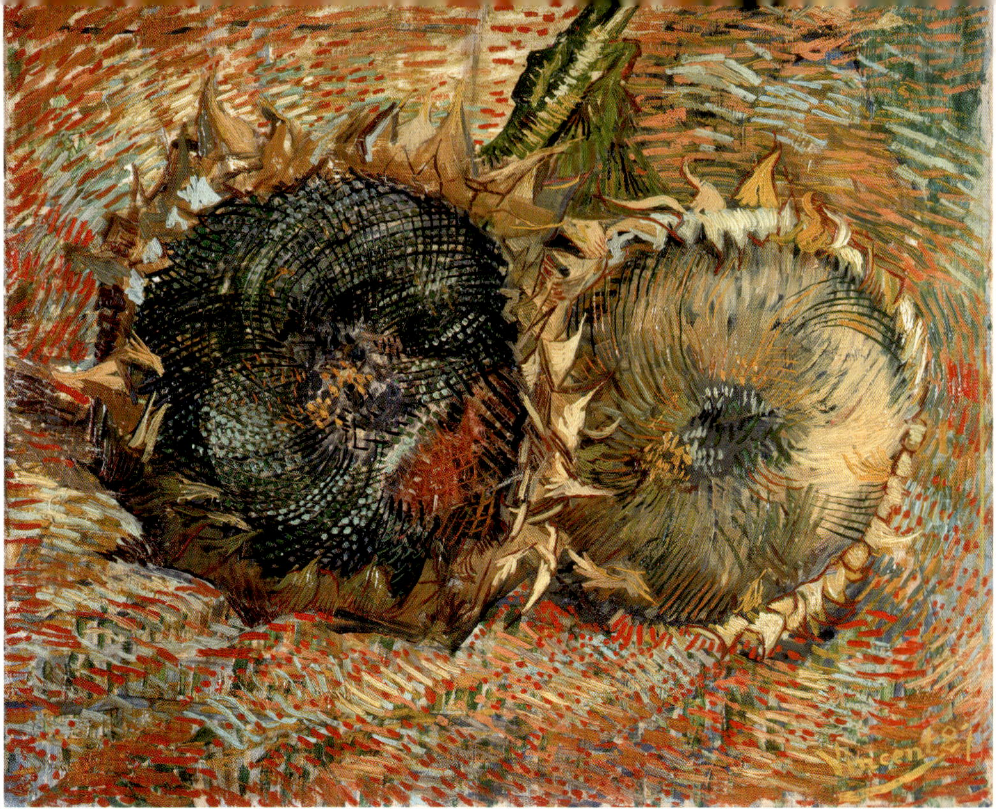

18
Vincent van Gogh
Sunflowers, 1887
Kunstmuseum, Bern

ground or a table, and that is what Van Gogh did here. Each of the four paintings is of two sunflower heads, apart from the last and largest canvas in the series, in which there are four. In the last three works he showed the flower heads from both above and below, as he had done similarly with the shoes in his still lifes of the year before (41).

In his first study of the sunflowers Van Gogh adopted a graphic approach (18) which was ideal for rendering the spiral arrangement of the seeds. In order to add variety to the two large sunflower heads he made the one on the left dark and the one on the right light, with the result that the latter tends to be swallowed up by the background. In a very small sketch he then examined the consequences of a new composition with a dark background (19). He now made the head on the left light, turned the other one around to show its back, and moved it a little further into the background. These simple adjustments greatly enlivened the composition, and he then repeated it in a second, much larger version (20). Initially he

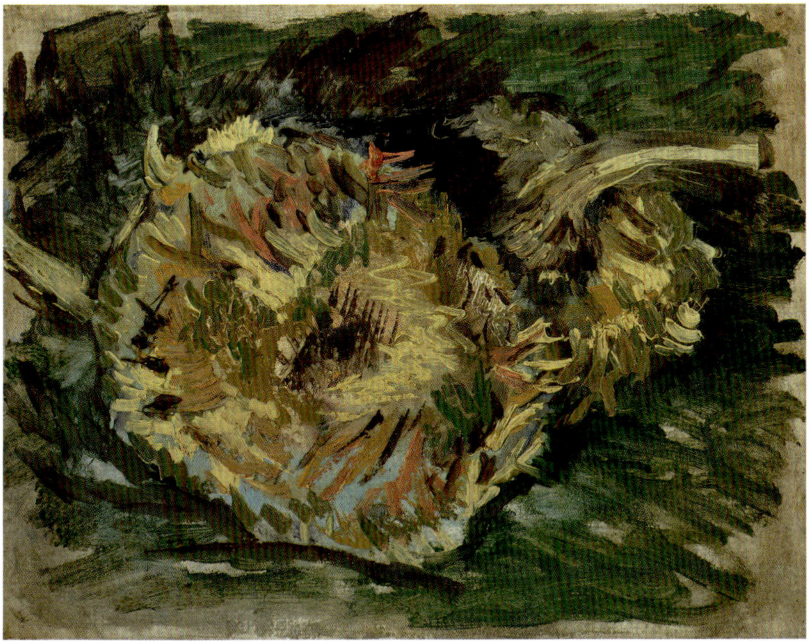

19
Vincent van Gogh
Sunflowers, 1887
Van Gogh Museum, Amsterdam

kept the background green, as in the preceding study, but then changed his mind and made it a bright blue.

The result was truly astounding. The colours have a powerful impact, partly due to the bright yellows, and Van Gogh decided to capitalize on this success in a much larger canvas with four instead of two sunflower heads (21). In this new painting he included more of the large, thick stems, stressing the robust nature of the plant. The enlargement of scale necessitated more variation in the background than in the previous painting, so in addition to blue he used contrasting oranges and related reds. He applied these colours with varied brushwork, and the result was highly intriguing. It is a feast for the eye of today's viewer familiar with the work of the twentieth-century Expressionists, but Van Gogh himself probably found it a little restless. He never finished it.

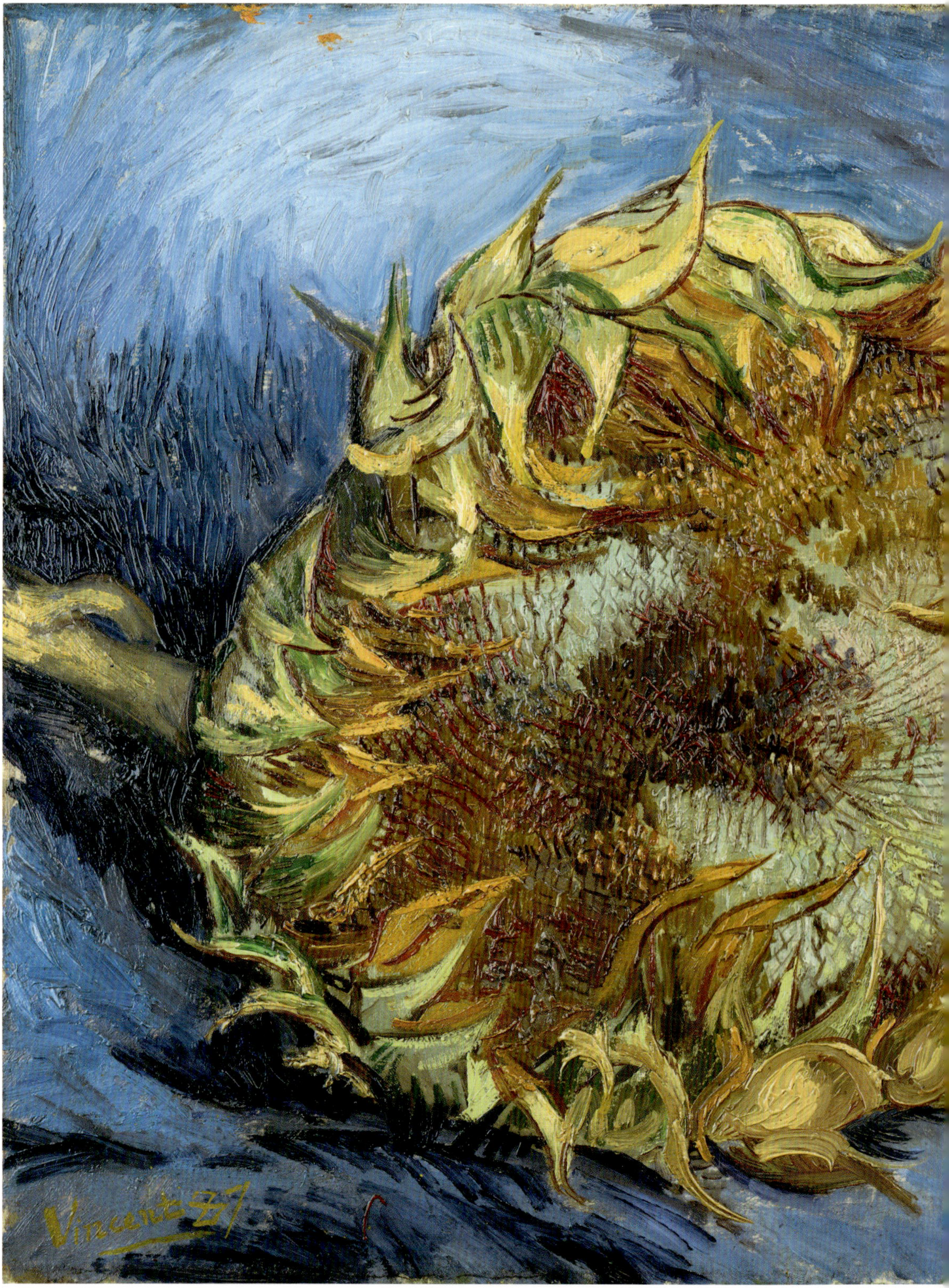
Vincent 87

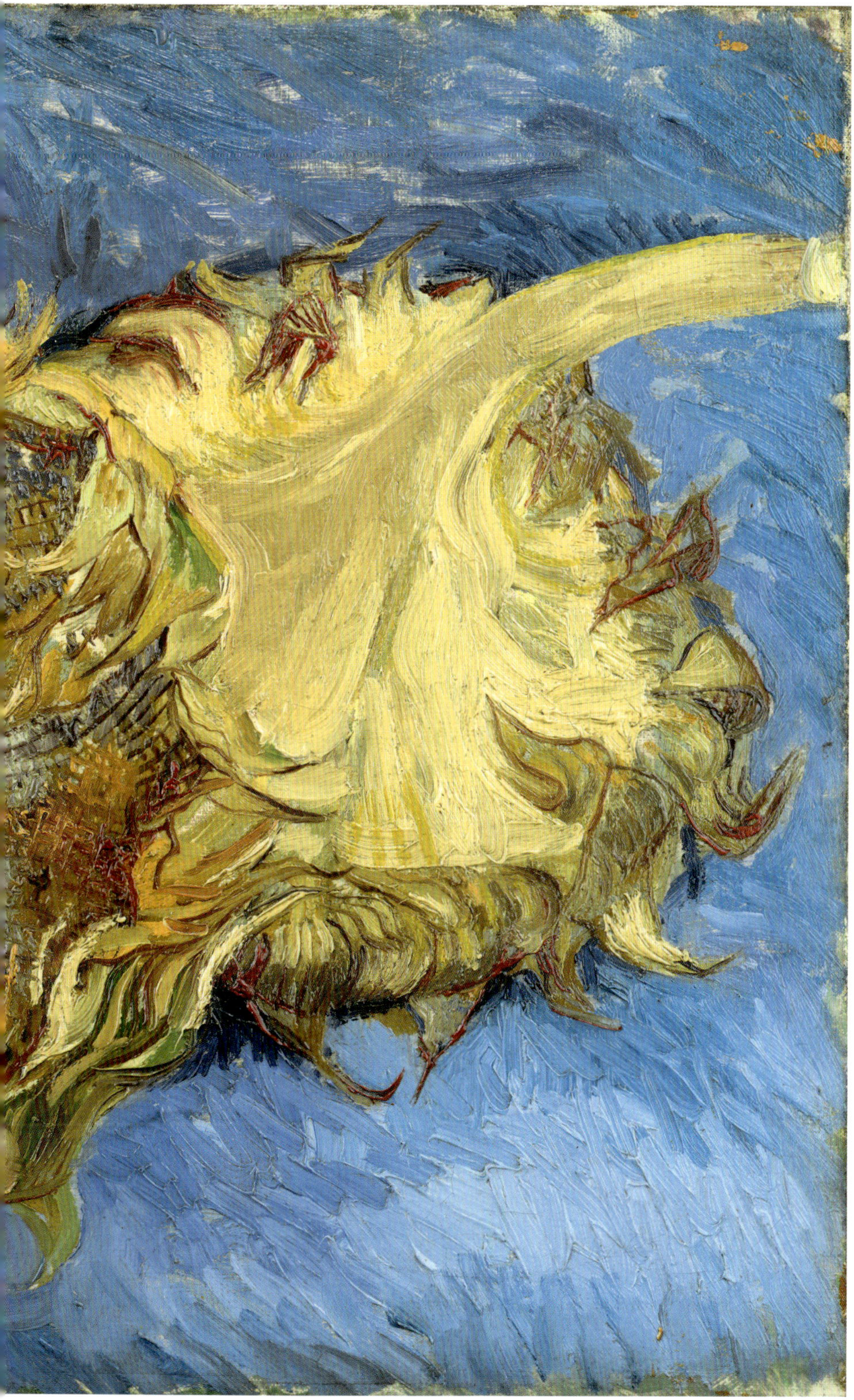

20
Vincent van Gogh
Sunflowers, 1887
The Metropolitan
Museum of Art,
New York

>21
Vincent van Gogh
Sunflowers, 1887
Kröller-Müller
Museum, Otterlo

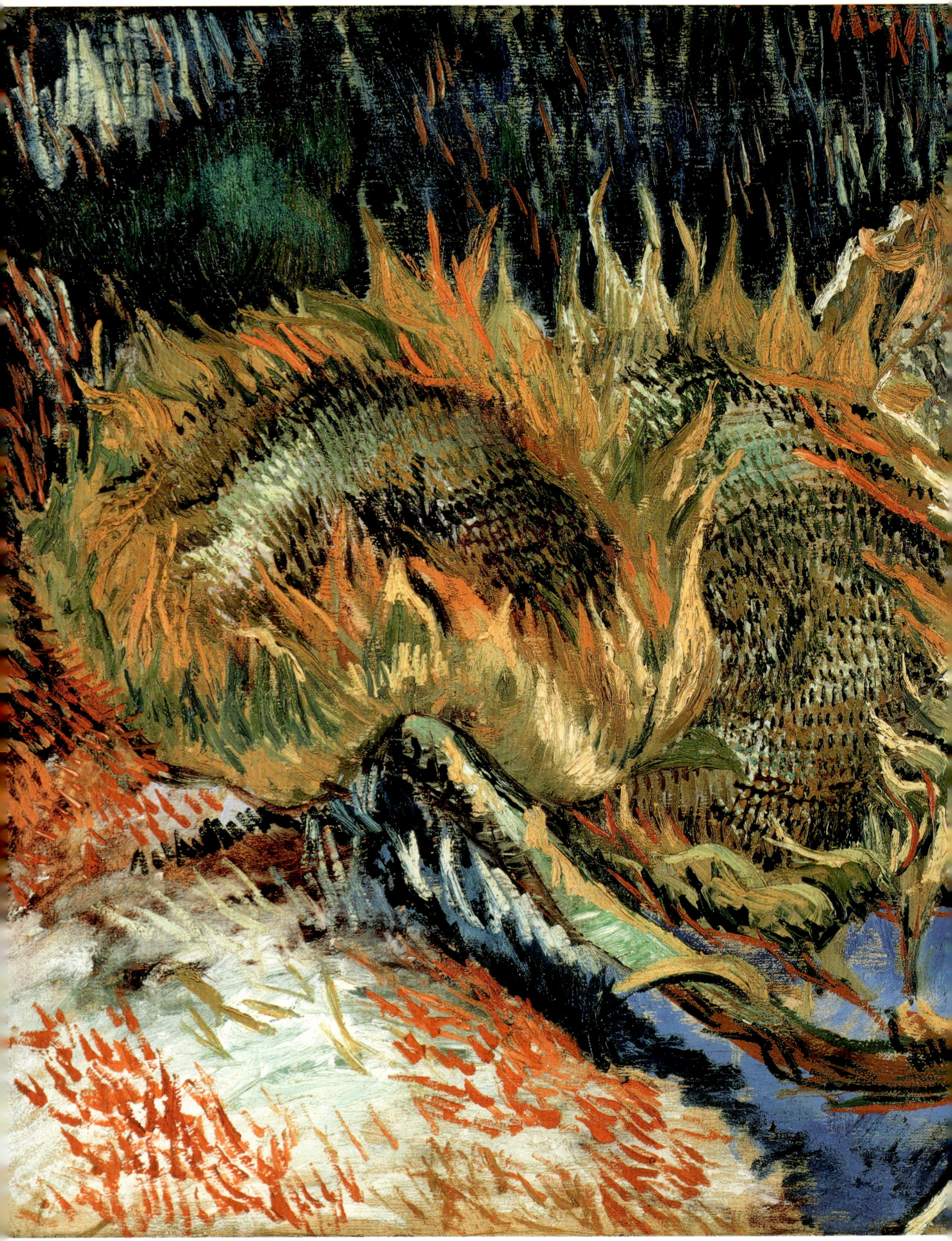

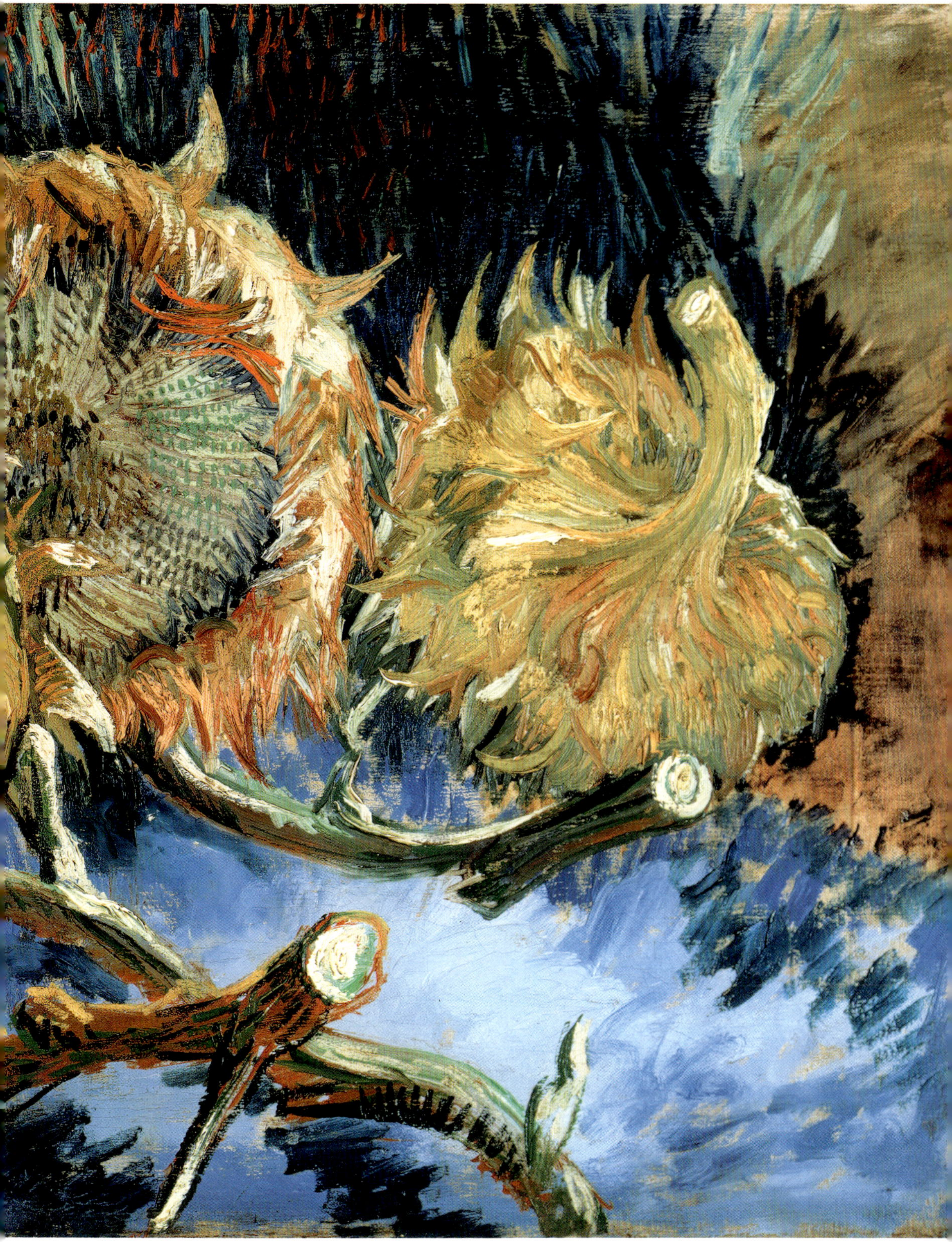

22
Maria van Oosterwijck
Bouquet with sunflower,
c. 1685
Staatliche Kunst-
sammlungen,
Gemäldegalerie Alte
Meister, Dresden

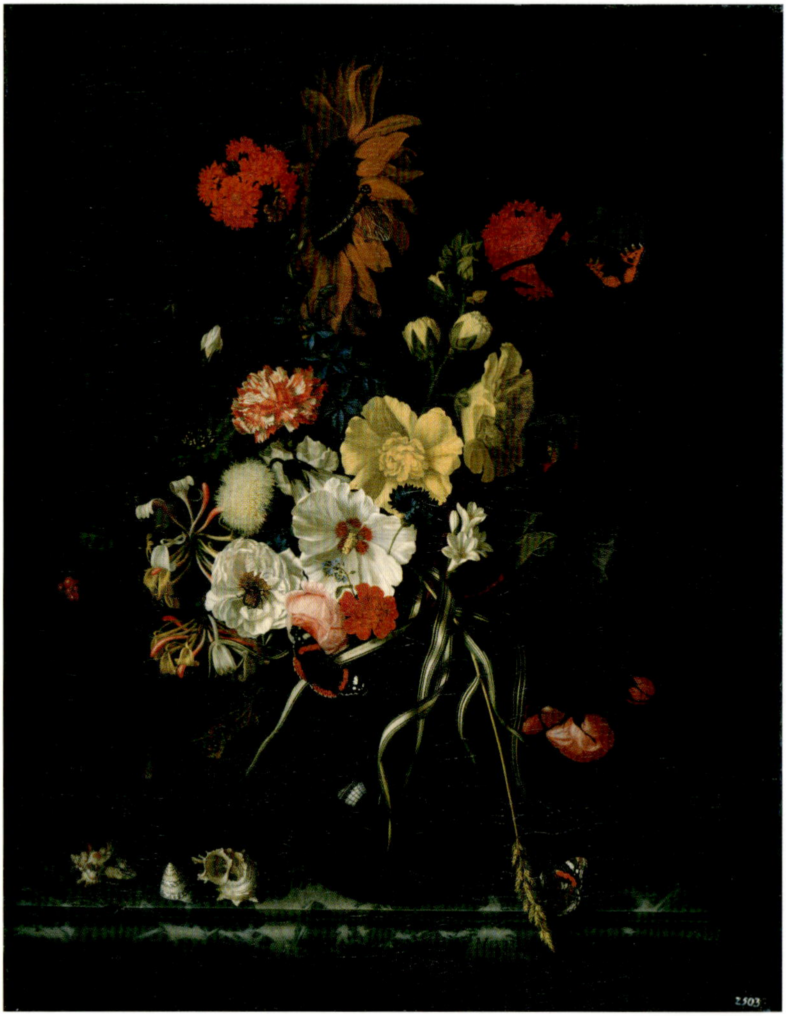

TRADITION

The sunflower was by no means as popular as the peony in still lifes of the time, but it had a respectable past. The first depictions of it date from the seventeenth century, when Dutch painters developed the genre of the flower piece. Their painted bouquets were intended as display pieces of the rarest kinds of flower, and some artists, like Maria van Oosterwijck, included the exotic sunflower as the crowning glory (22). This depiction

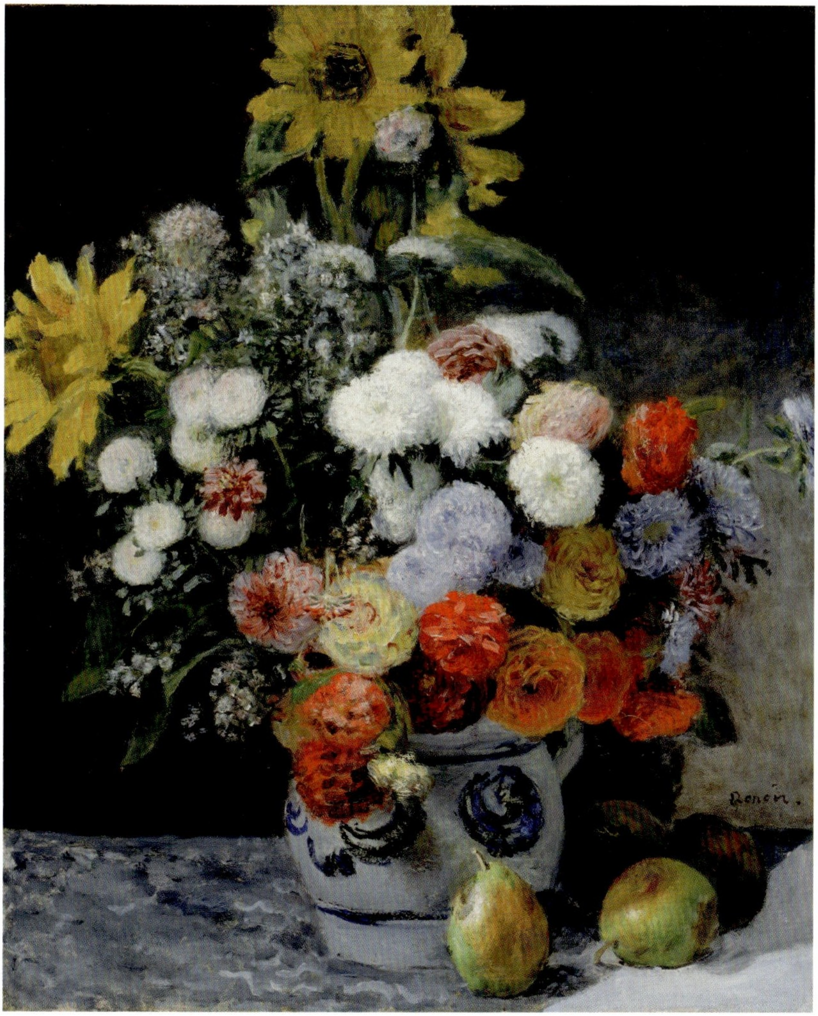

23
Auguste Renoir
Mixed flowers in an earthenware pot,
c. 1869
Museum of Fine Arts, Boston

of expensive flowers, some of which bloom at different times of the year, fell out of favour in the nineteenth century, and artists increasingly chose [illegible] show flowers which could be put in a vase at home, in other words cut flow[illegible] would be available at the same time, either from the market or from one[illegible] garden.

Sunflowers were [illegible]ally included in this new kind of flower piece. Their bright colour and large si[illegible] a little difficult to combine

24
Claude Monet
Still life with flowers and fruit, c. 1869
The J. Paul Getty Museum, Los Angeles

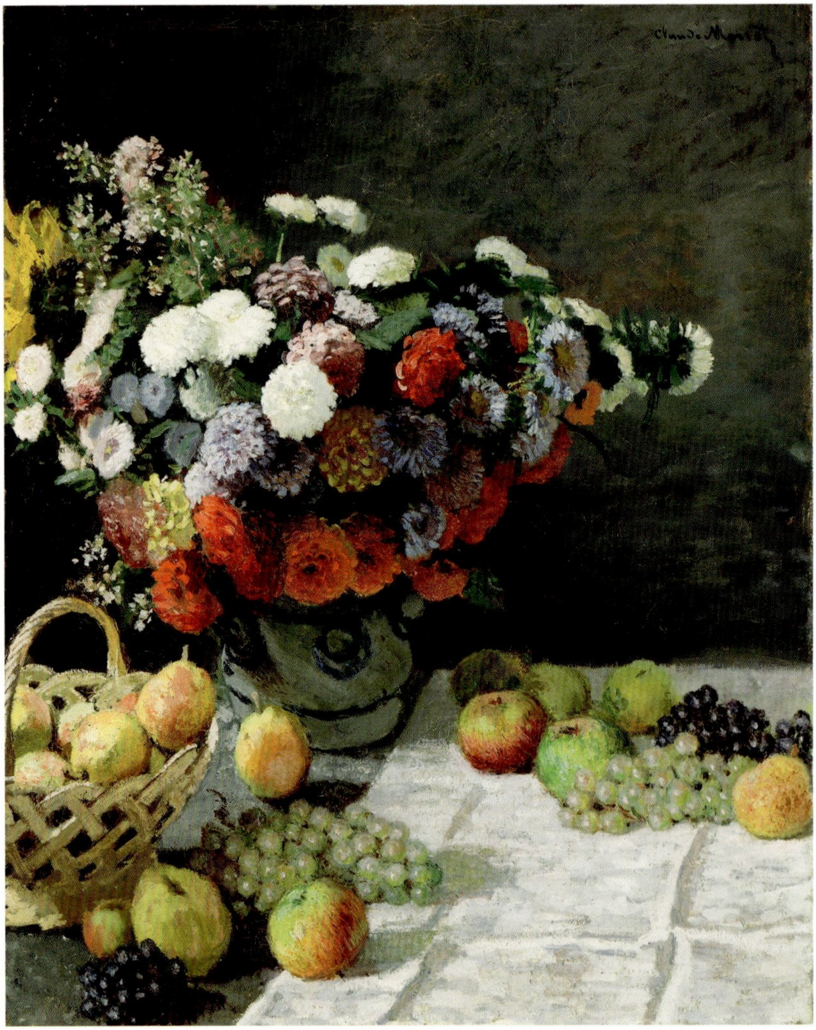

with other flowers, but some artists rose to the challenge. Monet and Renoir, for example, combined them mainly with chrysanthemums (23, 24), while Van Gogh grouped them with peonies and Chinese asters in his first year in Paris (25). Interestingly, unlike chrysanthemums, dahlias and peonies, sunflowers were rarely depicted in the form of a bouquet. They were considered unsuitable for display on their own. They were too large, too overpowering, too limited, which is probably why flower painters

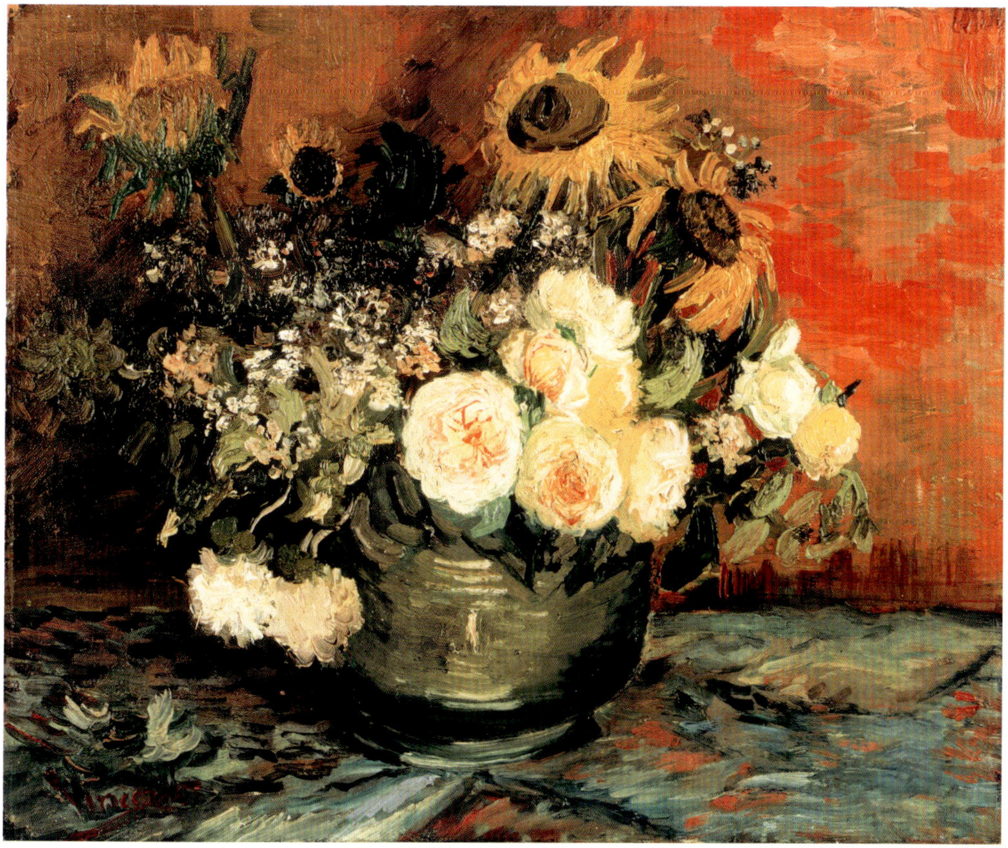

pur sang avoided them. Only a few non-specialists had the courage to take them on, among them Claude Monet, who painted a luxuriant bunch of sunflowers in a vase in 1881 (26). But this is an isolated example among his still lifes.

25
Vincent van Gogh
Vase of sunflowers, roses and other flowers, 1886
Städtische Kunsthalle, Mannheim

Van Gogh, in other words, was striking out on his own when he began focusing on sunflowers in 1887. He had 'taken the sunflower before others', as he later told Gauguin with barely concealed pride. What was truly original was the way in which he depicted it. Blooms were always shown in their full glory, but he preferred the sunflower when it was past its peak, displaying seeds and withered ray flowers. By contrast to other varieties, this stage in a sunflower's development was fascinating and

26
Claude Monet
Bouquet of sunflowers,
1881
The Metropolitan
Museum of Art,
New York

picturesque, and he made that the real subject of his still lifes. He was evidently not looking for appreciation from the average buyer of flower pieces but from 'people who are good observers of nature', as he had written two years before in connection with his unusual paintings of birds' nests.

One factor which may have influenced his decision to immerse himself or specialize in the sunflower was its popularity in the decorative arts in France. It had become a common motif in English decorative ensembles in the 1870s, and that taste, propagated largely by William Morris, crossed the Channel to France, where wallpaper decorated with sunflowers in the English fashion was quite common by the 1880s (27). We know that Van Gogh was very familiar with one particular decorative scheme with sunflowers, that in a branch of the Bouillon Duval, a chain of cheap eating-houses founded by the Parisian butcher Pierre Louis Duval. The restaurant was at 21 boulevard Montmartre, next door to the art gallery where Theo was the manager. Vincent referred to it in the late summer of 1888, when he came up with the plan of decorating his studio in Arles with still lifes of sunflowers. 'Next door to your shop', he wrote to Theo, 'in the restaurant, as you know, there is a lovely decoration of flowers. I always remember the big sunflower in the window there.'

Interestingly, Van Gogh painted his four still lifes with sunflowers in Paris just after he had lost his showcase for exhibiting his flower pieces, and there may have been a connection between the two events. In July 1887 Agostina Segatori, no longer now his lover, had lost her position as manageress of the Tambourin restaurant, which denied him any further opportunity of exhibiting there. When confronted with a setback, Van Gogh always looked for an alternative, and it is conceivable that he saw the Bouillon Duval in the boulevard Montmartre as a suitable new venue, if only because of the stream of visitors to Theo's gallery. This could have given him the idea of painting sunflowers. He may have thought that by matching his still lifes to the decoration of the restaurant he had more chance of persuading the manager to exhibit them. He was certainly not

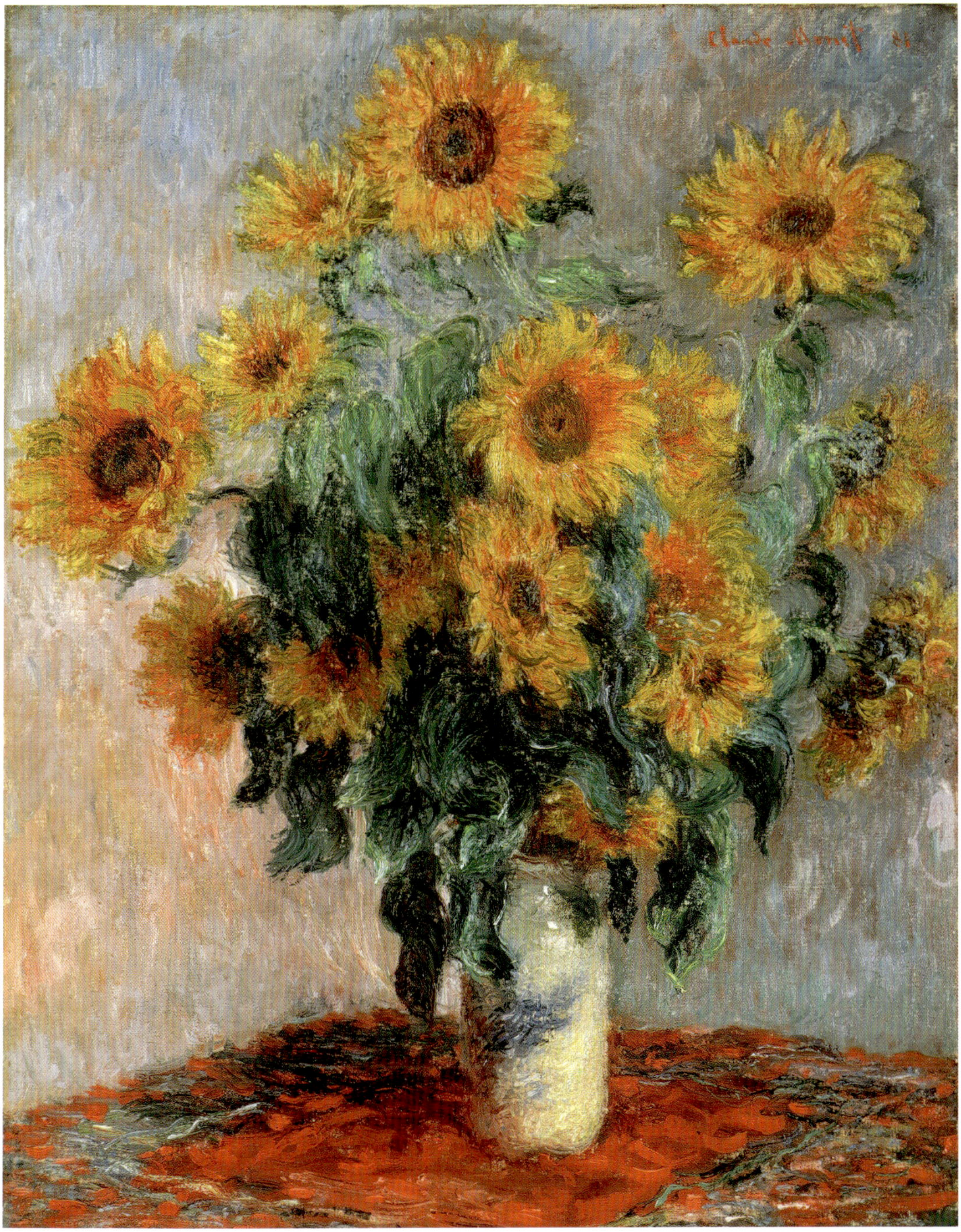
Claude Monet 81

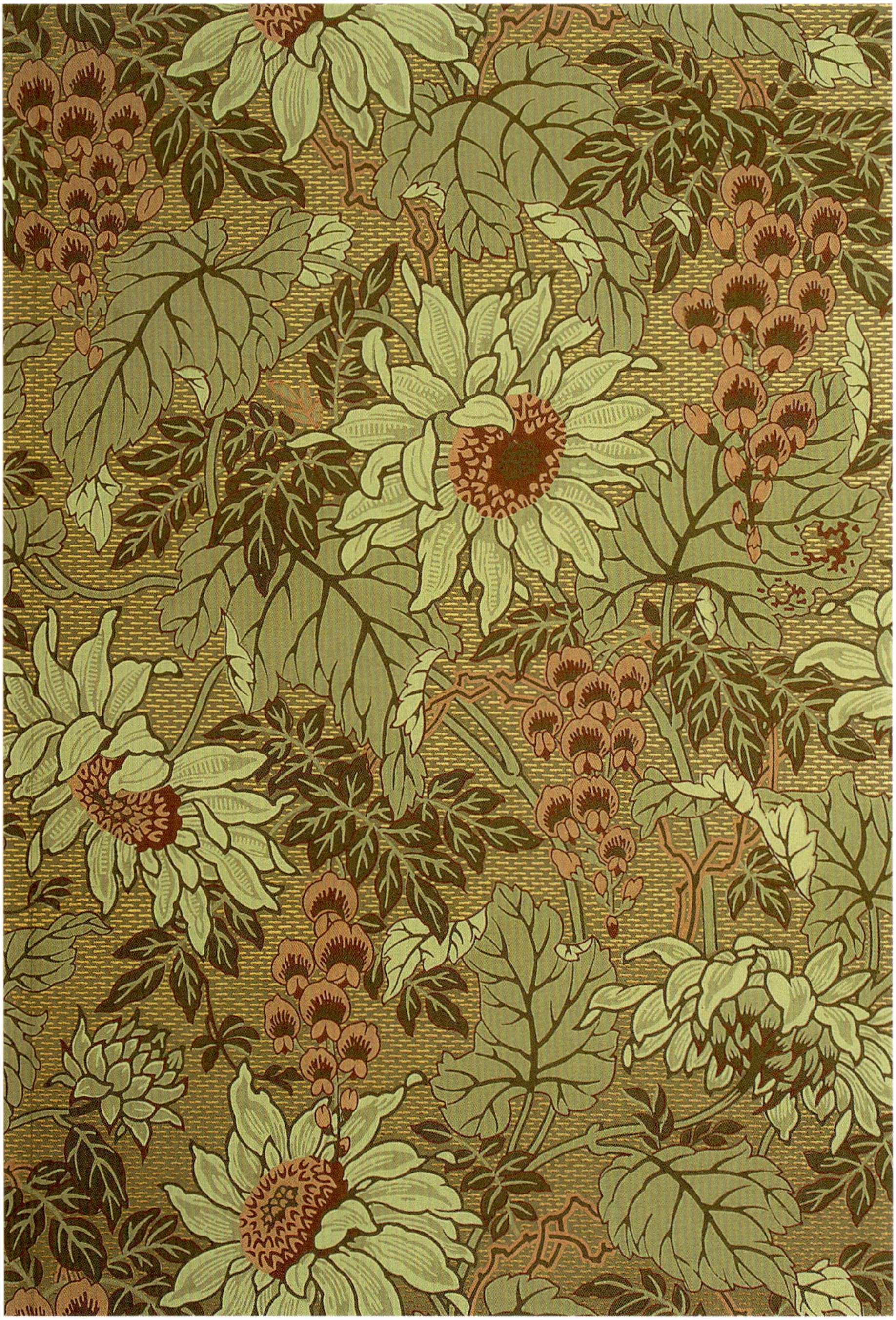

above this kind of opportunism, but, all the same, if he did try to put this plan into action, nothing came of it.

It was only in the autumn that he found a new exhibition space, when Étienne-Lucien Martin put at his disposal the dining room of his Grand Bouillon restaurant du Chalet at 43 avenue de Clichy, whereupon Van Gogh and several of his artist friends filled this restaurant-cum-*café concert* with their paintings. At least two of his sunflower still lifes hung there (18, 20), and to his delight he scored a success with them, for they caught the eye of Paul Gauguin, and although the two had only just met they decided to exchange works with each other. Although Gauguin obtained both still lifes, Van Gogh had to make do with just one painting, a recent work done in Martinique (28), which indicates just how self-effacing he was towards Gauguin.

27
Anonymous
Wallpaper with sunflowers, 1885
Musée du papier peint, Rixheim

28
Paul Gauguin
On the shore of the lake, Martinique, 1887
Van Gogh Museum, Amsterdam

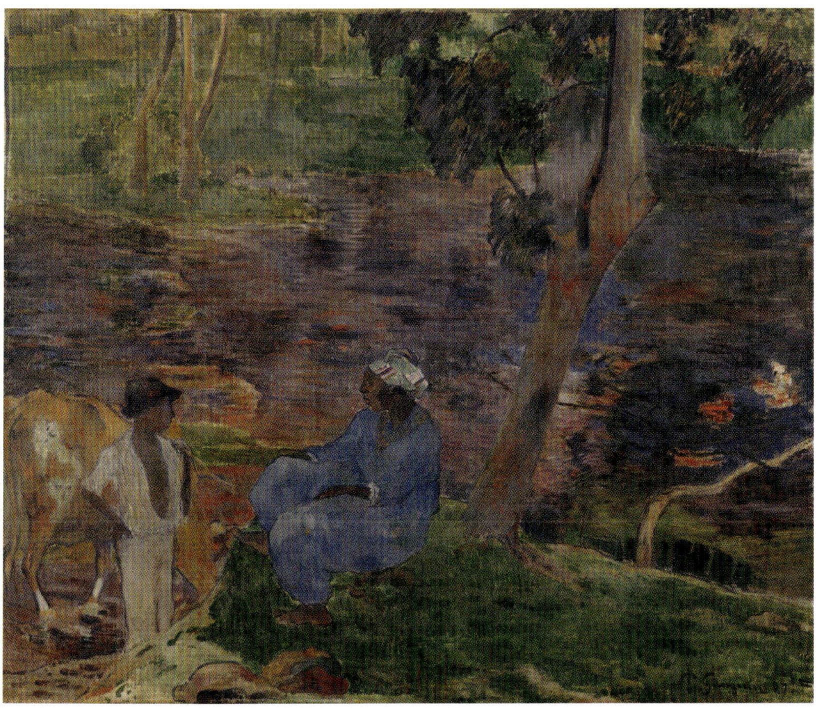

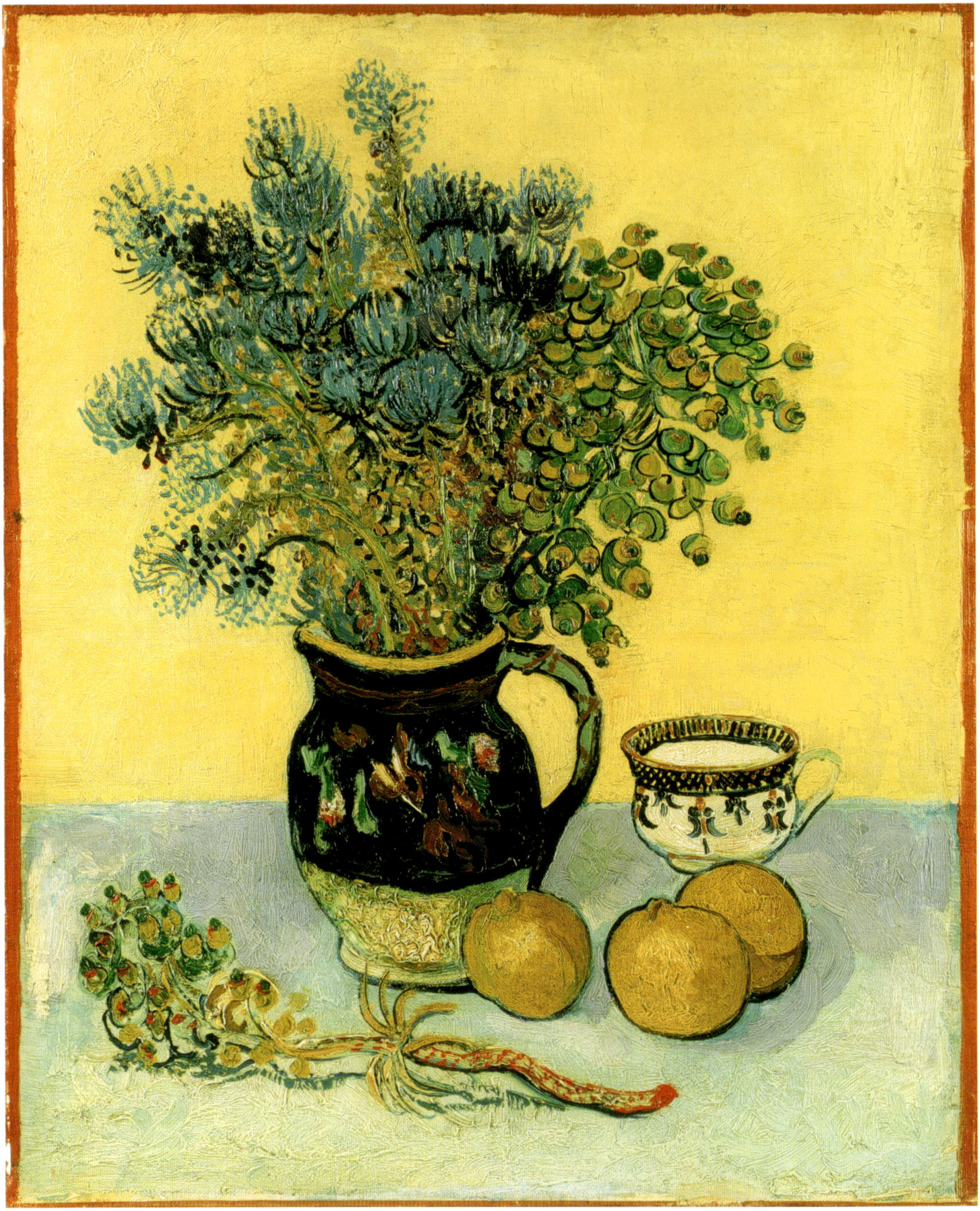

DECORATION

The exchange with Gauguin was very important to Van Gogh. He left for Arles at the beginning of 1888, and that summer he asked Gauguin if he would like to come and work with him in Provence. In his eyes, this was the cautious start of a community of artists, the purpose of which was to profit from one another's knowledge and experience. Gauguin, who was in Brittany at the time, accepted the offer, but left Van Gogh in the dark as to when he would actually be coming. It was perhaps in order to convince him of his good intentions and hurry him up that in August Van Gogh hit on the idea of decorating his studio in the Yellow House with 'Nothing but large sunflowers', knowing that Gauguin liked the subject.

He thought of painting six still lifes of them, but later increased the total to twelve. He wanted to make 'a decoration in which the raw or broken chrome yellows will blaze forth on various BLUE backgrounds, from the palest Veronese to *royal blue*, framed in thin strips of wood painted with orange lead. Effects like those of *stained-glass windows* in a Gothic church', as he wrote to Émile Bernard, another artist friend who was with Gauguin in Brittany at the time. This soon led to the plan to decorate the entire Yellow House with paintings, the underlying idea being to turn it into an exhibition space – a new showcase for his art, as Le Tambourin had been in Paris.

At this point Van Gogh had only painted a few still lifes in Arles. He had depicted wild flowers (29), oleanders, asters and marigolds, but it was not until August that he felt like concentrating on the genre. That was after he had seen the garden of a local bathhouse (31) and a small but very colourful peasant's garden (30), in which the flowers vibrated 'like the bouquet by Monticelli which you have' (7), as he wrote to Theo. There were tall sunflowers standing in both gardens, and it was shortly afterwards that he started on his ambitious programme of decorations.

Van Gogh gave a detailed account of his progress in his letters. Sunflowers fade fast, and he wrote that it was best to do the planned series of twelve 'in one rush'. Although he worked with 'the enthusiasm of a

29
Vincent van Gogh
Still life, 1888
The Barnes Foundation, Merion, PA

>30
Vincent van Gogh
Garden with flowers, 1888
Private collection

>31
Vincent van Gogh
Garden of a bathhouse, 1888
Van Gogh Museum, Amsterdam

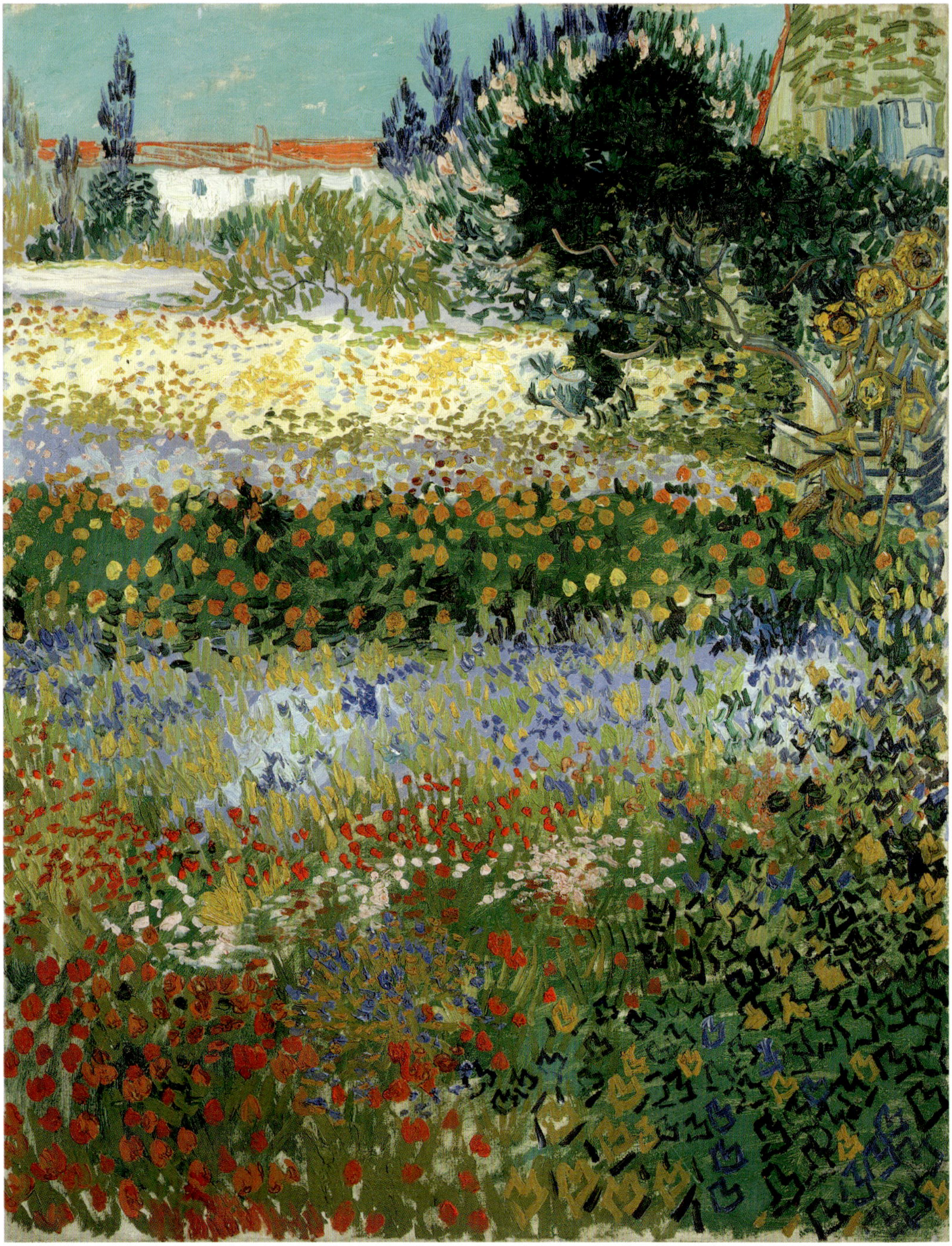

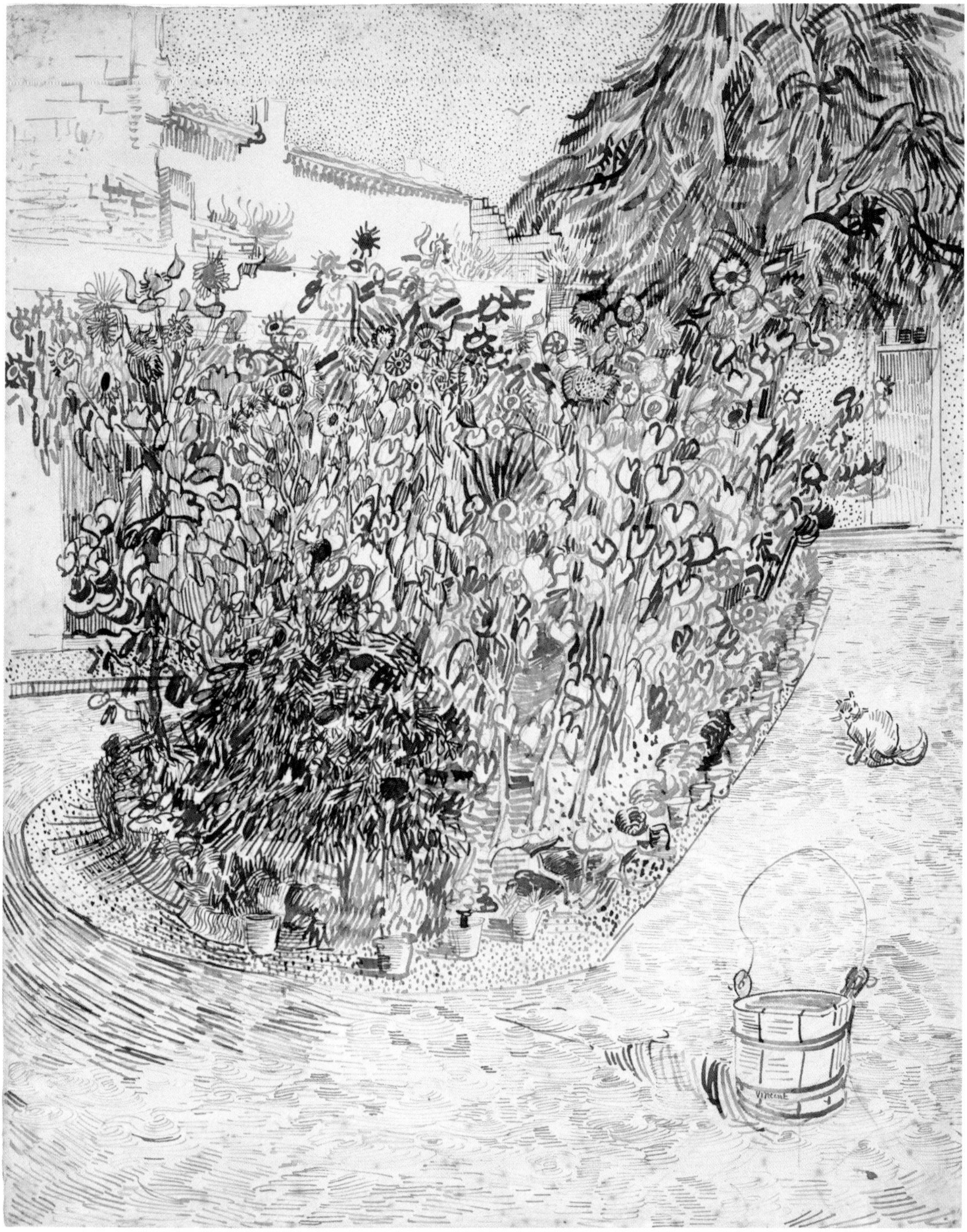

32
Antique French green-glazed preserving jar

33
Antique Provençal preserving jar with partial yellow glaze

Marseillais eating bouillabaisse', he did not manage to paint six, let alone twelve, before the flowering season was over, but just four – two small ones and two large (34–37). This time, by contrast to his Paris sunflowers, he opted for a conventional composition with the vase, a typical piece of domestic Provençal earthenware, in the middle. In the first two paintings it is a vase glazed entirely green apart from the foot (32), and in the second two it is a vase glazed yellow at the top with a rough lower half (33).

Van Gogh started by carefully portraying three flowers (34), two still in full bloom and one at a later stage. He developed that scene in his next study (35), adding two heads with stems in the foreground, one before it had flowered and one after. What is more important is that he now used a different visual vocabulary, that of Japanese prints. During his time in Paris, his friend Bernard had urged him to take that art as his model, and here he stuck to that rigidly. He used emphatic contours, marked colour contrasts and a decorative distribution of surfaces, and used dark royal blue for the background. In this way he indeed achieved the effect of a stained-glass window.

He was not happy with the result. For his third, much larger painting, he decided not to be so stylized, and reverted to 'simplicity of technique' (36), which was a radical change of approach. For his brushwork he

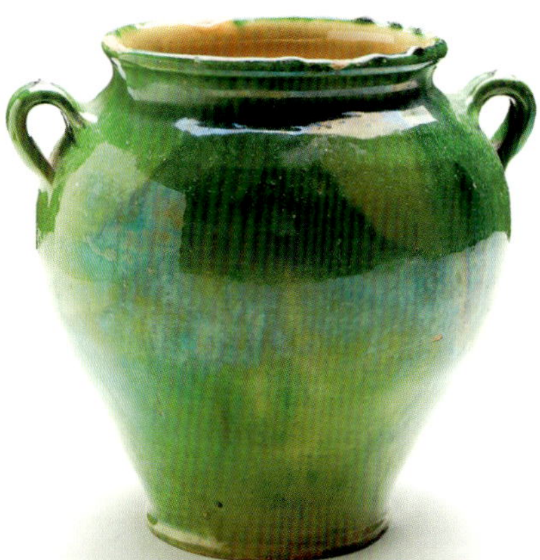

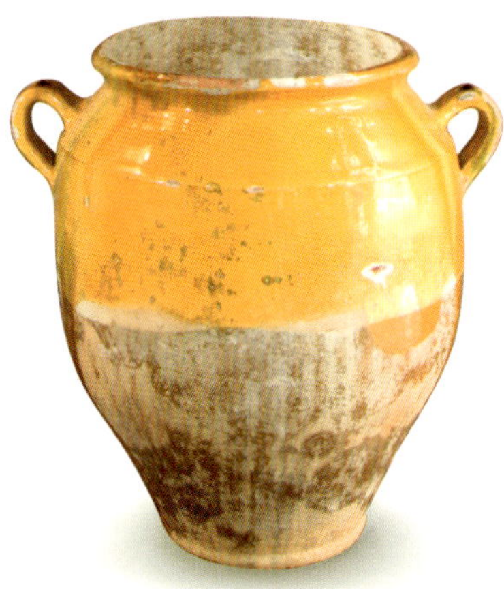

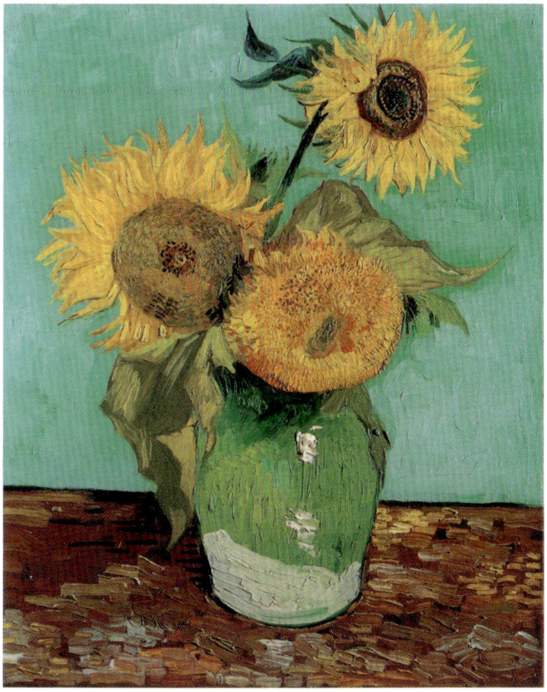

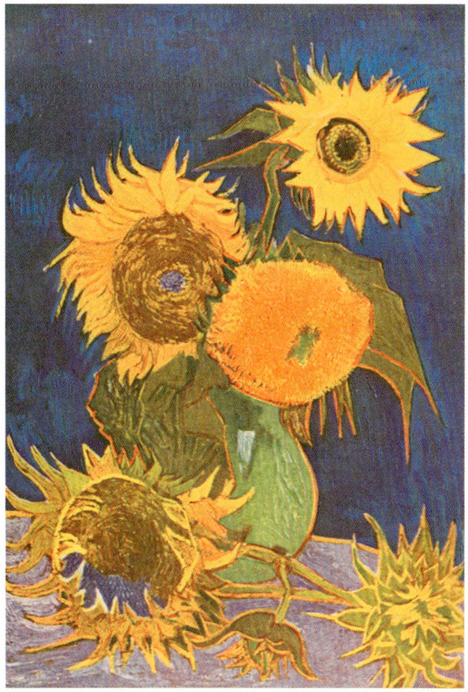

adopted 'the varied stroke', which was a reference to the airy manner of Manet's *Peonies in a vase* (6) that he admired so much. Striving for colour contrasts was replaced by seeking a 'light on light' effect, which gives a very definitely decorative impression, as in the preceding painting. It is true that his main colours remained blue and yellow, but he used hardly any contrasts between light and shade. The composition is much more ambitious, for now there are no fewer than fourteen flowers in the vase. He depicted them from different angles, from the front, the side, and even one from the back, and as before he combined flowering heads with others that were past their prime.

34
Vincent van Gogh
Sunflowers, 1888
Private collection

35
Vincent van Gogh
Sunflowers, 1888
Lost in the Second World War

Van Gogh perfected the scene he had now arrived at in his equally large fourth still life, in which he increased the number of flowers to sixteen (37). He succeeded in making the composition airier than in the previous work, with the large, overblown blooms coalescing into a large cluster. He placed three of them at the bottom and three at the top, and

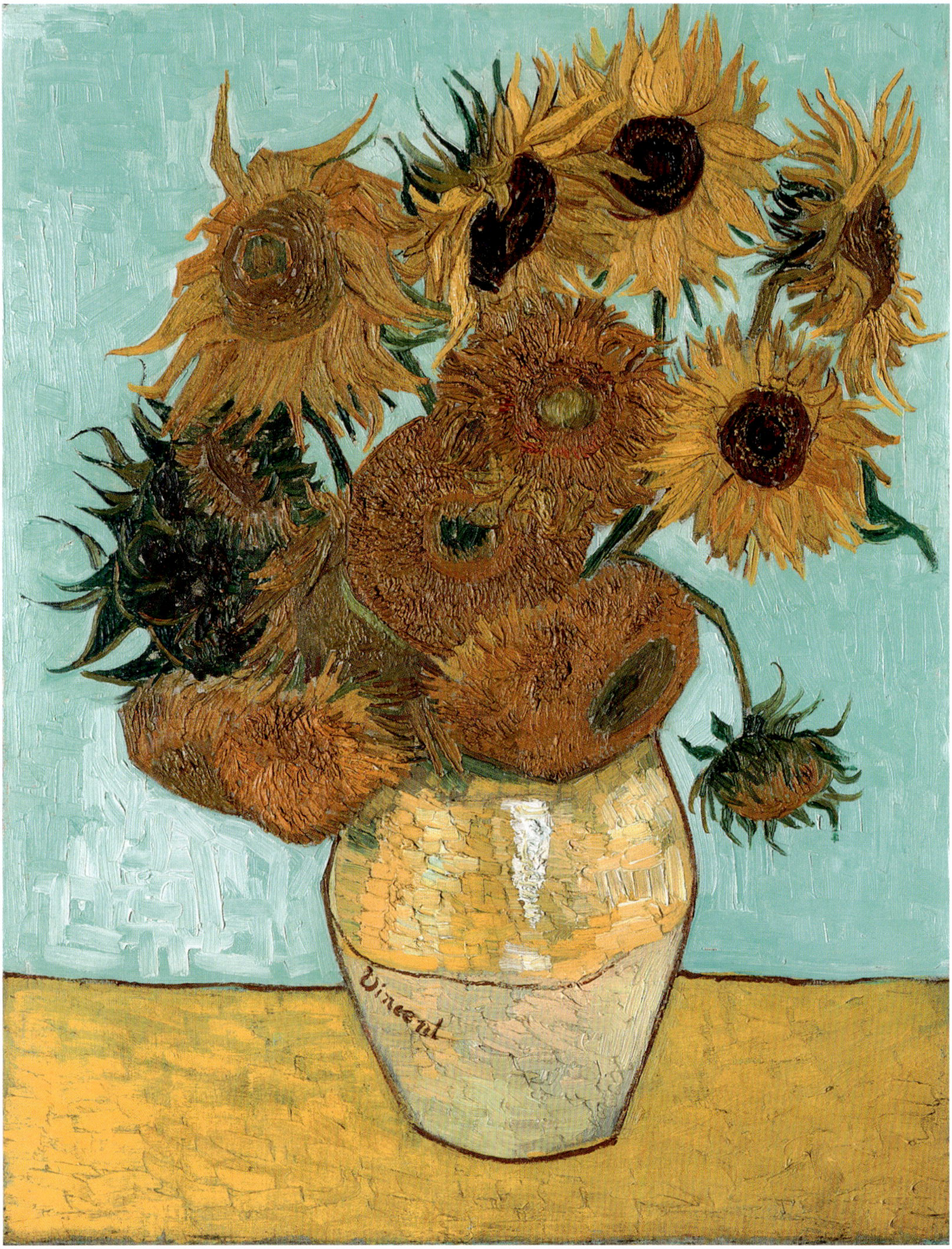

36 Vincent van Gogh, *Sunflowers*, 1888, Neue Pinakothek, Munich

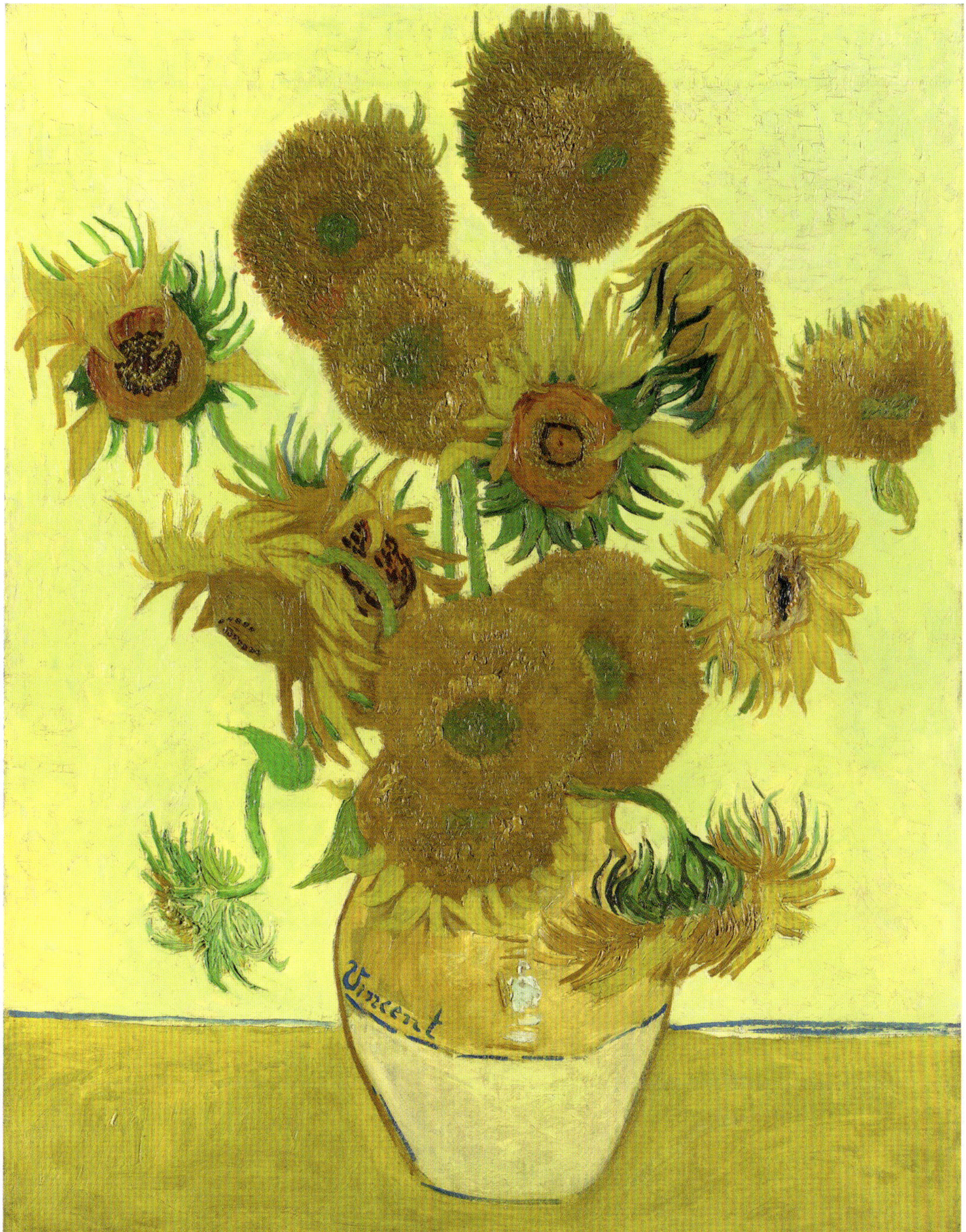

37 Vincent van Gogh, *Sunflowers*, 1888, The National Gallery, London

38
Vincent van Gogh
Still life with quinces, lemons, pears and grapes, 1887
Van Gogh Museum, Amsterdam

allowed the background to show through the gaps in the bouquet. By choosing heads that were going to seed as the crowning motifs, he placed far more emphasis on the withering process than in the other paintings, and that was probably his intention. He also added a new element. Sunflowers have distinctive, sinuous stems, which he captured superbly in the flowers at the very bottom.

Van Gogh's handling of his brush had become more refined. In his search for 'the varied stroke' he even included flat, thin passages – in the vase, the foreground and most of the ray flowers. He improved the 'light on light' effect by reducing the contrast of light and shade between the background and the subject. For example, he made the reddish brown

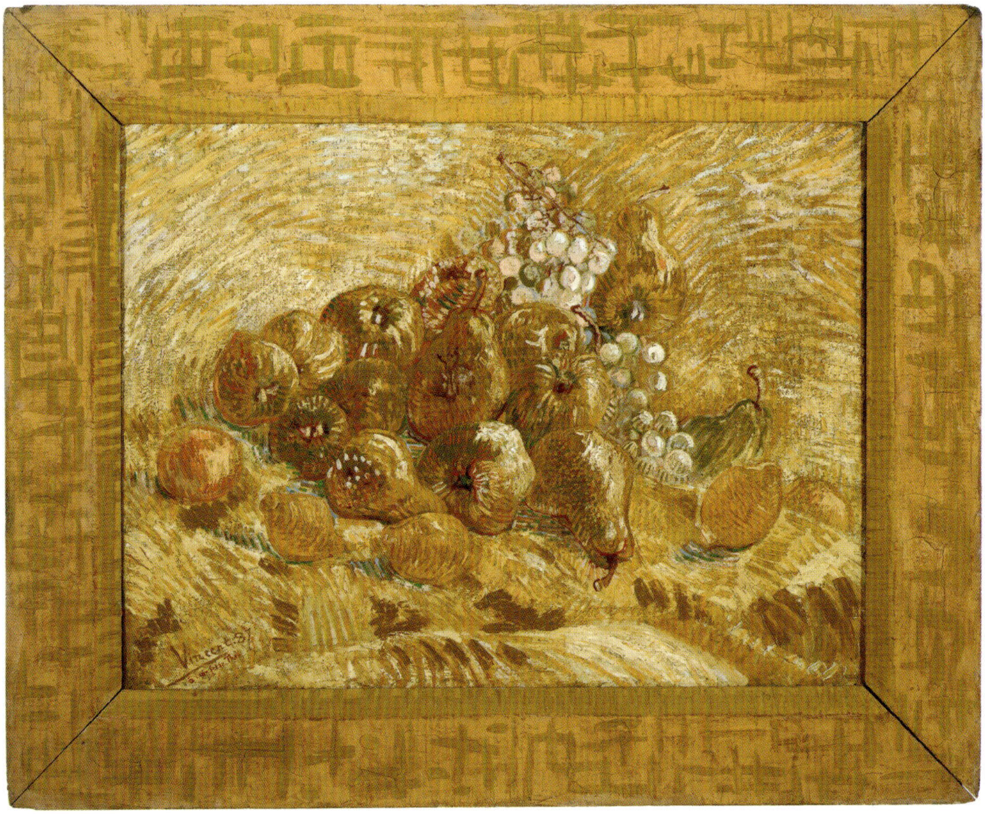

hearts of some of the flowers less prominent, and painted the leaves with light instead of dark green. The background, too, is no longer turquoise mixed with white, but a light yellow, which because of its natural tonal value is of course a better option for painting light on light.

Van Gogh thus abandoned his original plan of allowing yellow and blue to dominate the series. Experimenting as he went along, he had changed those main colours into 'the three chrome yellows, yellow ochre and malachite green, and nothing else'. The still life thus grew into a display of technical virtuosity. He demonstrated that it was possible to use many variants of a single colour within a scene without losing pictorial richness and form. He tellingly compared this work with the *Still life with lemons and quinces* that he had painted in Paris (38), which is also mainly in yellow tones, but in which the brushwork is far less direct and loose.

One may not notice it at first glance, but compared to his Paris still lifes of the motif Van Gogh was not now trying to produce a morphologically accurate portrait of the sunflowers. For example, in his first study (34) he gave the overblown bloom at bottom right a green heart, and he did the same for the faded flowers in the larger canvases (36, 37). It was a very strange choice of colour. Heads that have almost finished flowering are a yellowish brown, and in the centre they are a little darker, at most. Van Gogh depicted this by adding an accent, but he probably opted for the unrealistic green in order to set up a contrast with the other heads that had not yet finished flowering, the hearts of which are an orangey brown. Something that is equally unnatural is the flowering head in the centre of the bouquet in the final still life (37). Van Gogh needed green here to break through the dominant yellow, and simply left out half of the ray flowers in order to reveal the underlying sepals.

Although the composition or bouquet looks natural, it too would have been manipulated. In the first painting of the series (34) we see sunflowers with short stems, and this is undoubtedly true to life. The heads of the flowers are large and heavy, and the short stems are the reason why the vase has not become top-heavy and toppled over. In the last two paintings, however, the stems are long and there are a lot of flowers in the vase, which shows that these bouquets were not painted from life but were put together on the canvas. Combined with the morphological discrepancies mentioned above, this makes the last still lifes a fine example of his statement that he was a realist who did not stick to the literal truth: 'I exaggerate, sometimes I make changes in the motif; but for all that I do not invent the whole picture; on the contrary, I find it all ready in nature, only it must be disentangled.'

MEANING

For connoisseurs, there was and is much to experience in the last painting in the series (37). With his bold use of colour and sculptural brushwork, Van Gogh had worked in the spirit of the admired Monticelli (7), but succeeded in combining the roughness of this almost unknown master with the airiness and simplicity of Manet (6) – and that was quite an achievement when one considers the great differences between those two painters. The shapes of the flowers look a little primitive here and there, which may have been done to please Gauguin, who had recently told him that he and Bernard were trying to 'paint like children'. Since Van Gogh had also honoured his friends' demand to think more in terms of areas of solid colour, following the example of Japanese woodcuts, he had every reason to be proud of his work.

'Now to get up heat enough to melt that gold, those flower tones, it isn't everybody who can do it, it needs the whole and entire force and concentration of a single individual', he later wrote. He assured Theo that 'one of those Scotsmen or Americans' would be prepared to pay 500 francs for each of the last two still lifes (36, 37), which would mean that they were worth as much as Theo's flower painting by Monticelli. However, he did realise that he had made this great achievement in a low, essentially commercial genre. It was only when he could embody the qualities of these still lifes in a figure painting that he would 'have a position in art equal to that of anyone, no matter who'.

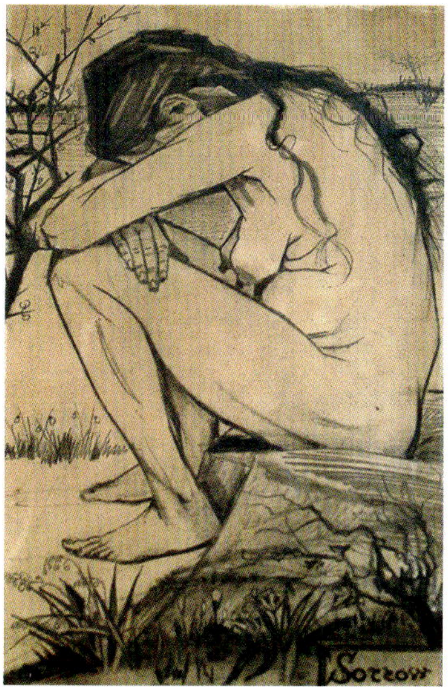

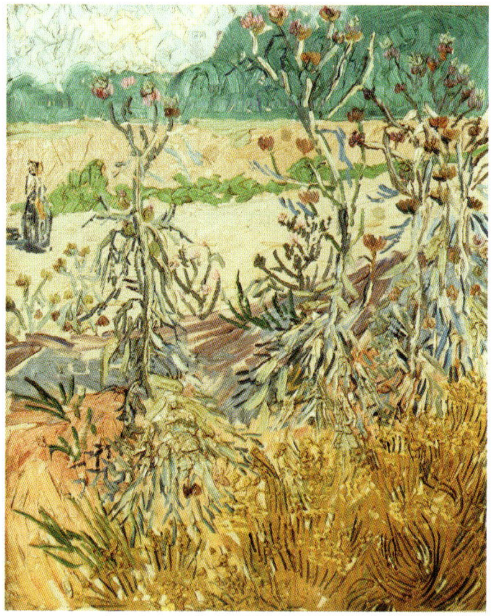

39
Vincent van Gogh
Sorrow, 1882
The New Art Gallery, Walsall, The Garman Ryan Collection

40
Vincent van Gogh
Thistles, 1888
Private collection

41
Vincent van Gogh
Three pairs of shoes, 1886
Fogg Art Museum, Cambridge (Mass.)

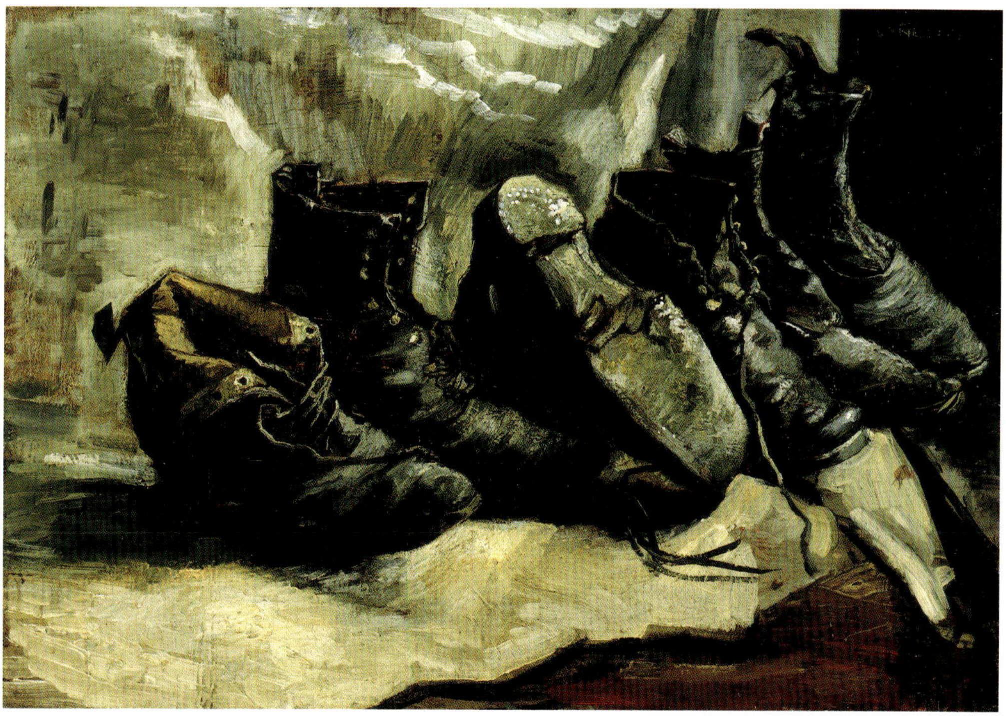

42
Vincent van Gogh
Portrait of Madame Trabuc, 1889
The State Hermitage Museum, St Petersburg

It might seem, then, that the picturesque sunflowers, some of which are going to seed, were nothing more than an excuse for Van Gogh to enable his pictorial talents to blossom, but nothing could be further from the truth. His choice, back in 1887, to show flowers not just in all their finery but also in a state of decay was by no means an arbitrary one. He had been formed as an artist by Realism, and that movement had called classical beauty superficial. Artists had to seek out their subjects 'close to the ground', and in line with this new aesthetic he developed a preference for things 'over which life has passed', as he put it so strikingly in 1881. That applied also to his sunflowers. These flowers, literally found in the ground, had 'nothing distinguished, nothing extraordinary, nothing unusual' about them, but did have the endless charm of 'that slight fadedness, that something over which life has passed'. Although he wrote those words in 1883 about his older lover Sien Hoornik, who had been hurt by life and is depicted as such in *Sorrow* (39), they are just as applicable to the wilting sunflowers in his still lifes from both Paris and Arles.

The expressiveness that Van Gogh was looking for in his *Sunflowers* was no different from that in his many still lifes of down-at-heel and muddy shoes, in which he also celebrated the beauty of old, everyday objects (41). There is also a certain affinity with *Thistles* (40), which he painted in Arles just before his sunflower series. He depicted these roadside plants, which are even less prestigious than sunflowers, in flower and withering. He called them 'dusty', and we know what associations that held for him from a letter written in Saint-Rémy. In it he described Jeanne Trabuc, the wife of the chief orderly of the mental asylum, as 'a faded woman, an unhappy, resigned creature of small account, so insignificant that I have a great longing to paint that dusty blade of grass', which he then proceeded to do (42).

Van Gogh's interest in such simple subjects marked by a hard existence was based on the idea that they would express the essence and above all tragedy of life. As such they provided consolation, but in Arles,

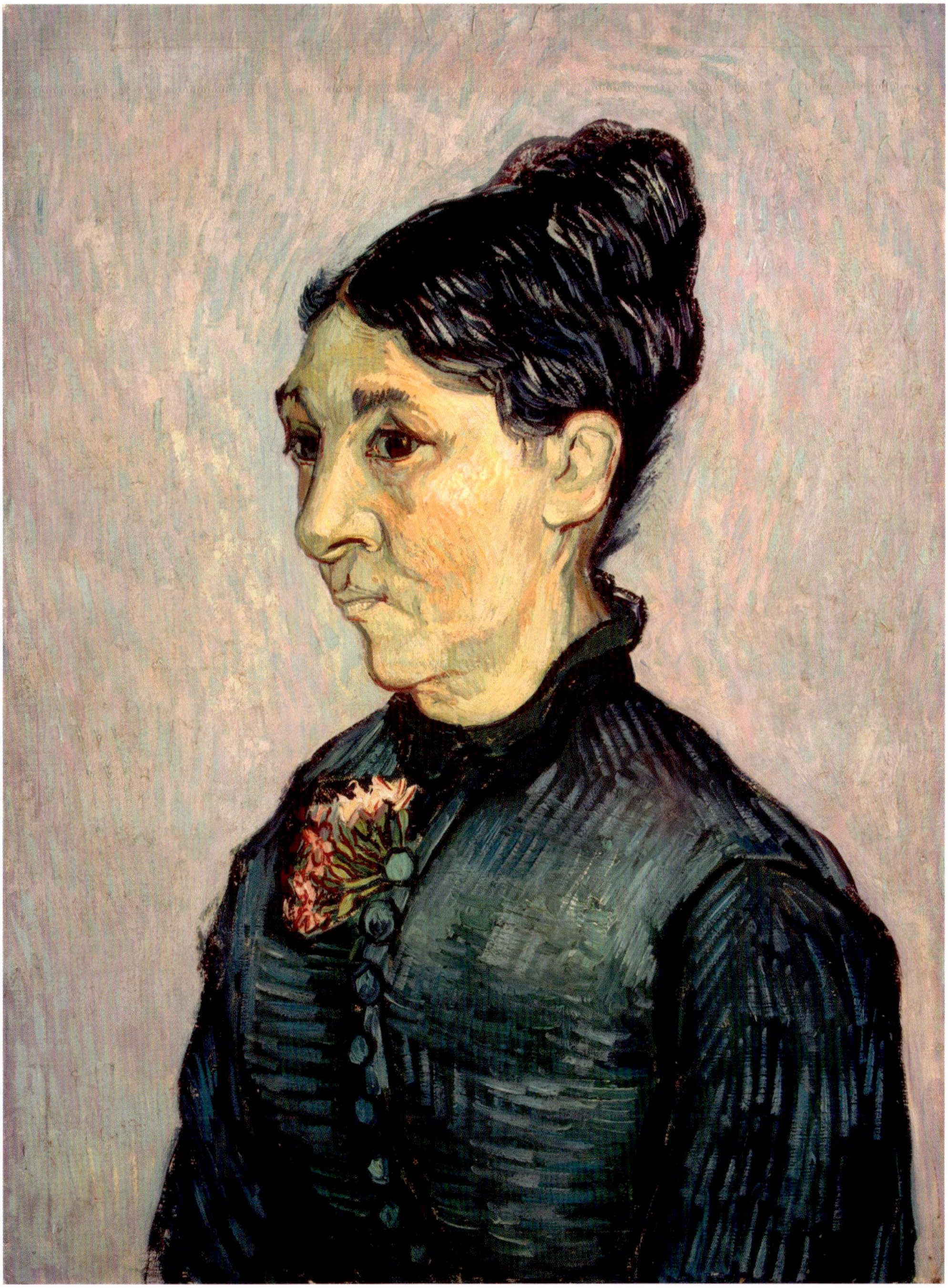

in contrast to his Dutch period, he no longer felt that that consolation came from the subject alone. He was increasingly coming to believe that the *form* was responsible for that evocation, and in particular the colouring. In a painting he wanted 'to say something comforting, as music is comforting. I want to paint men and women with that something of the eternal which the halo used to symbolize, and which we seek to convey by the actual radiance and vibration of our colouring.' As applied to the *Sunflowers*, this means that Van Gogh would have regarded the successful colouring, from bright orange to pale yellow, as 'comforting music'. Because he made his still lifes to decorate his studio, we can assume that he saw them as symbolic of the direction he believed the planned community of artists should take. He evidently believed that Gauguin shared that higher ideal of comforting art. Or, as he wrote in early 1889 after the failure of their collaboration, 'Oh, dear friend, to make of painting what the music of Berlioz and Wagner has been before us ... an art that comforts sorrowful hearts. There are only a few who feel that in the way you and I do!!!'

COLLABORATION WITH GAUGUIN

After having painted four still lifes, Van Gogh abandoned his plan of using the sunflowers to decorate his studio. With the prospect of Gauguin coming to stay he decided to decorate the Yellow House from top to bottom, and he installed the two large ones (36, 37) in 'the prettiest room upstairs'. This was the small guest room, Gauguin's, which he intended to furnish with 'elegance', 'like the boudoir of a really artistic woman'. This may sound an odd thing to say, but it was prompted by Van Gogh's desire to make the room fit the character of his guest. In his eyes, Gauguin was a true genius, and in those days that meant that he was blessed with a sensitive, feminine nature. So flowers, however rustic and commonplace, were as fitting as the rocking chair he bought for his colleague. All of this was in marked contrast to his own bedroom (43), which he wanted to keep extremely simple, in line with his view of his own qualities as an artist.

When Gauguin arrived at the end of October he said that the two still lifes of sunflowers, along with the *Bedroom* (43) and *Sower*, were 'really beautiful', Van Gogh proudly reported. His guest preferred the yellow version of the *Sunflowers* (37) to the blue one (36), and after a month set the pair of them the task of studying the question of 'the orchestration of a pure colour by all the derivatives of that colour', as he later put it. For this purpose Gauguin painted 'a large still life of an orange-coloured pumpkin, apples and white linen on a yellow background and foreground', which Van Gogh found superb. Gauguin, though, did not, and after he left Arles he cut it to pieces, keeping only a horizontal strip which he partly overpainted by adding a cat (45).

43
Vincent van Gogh
Bedroom, 1888
Van Gogh Museum, Amsterdam

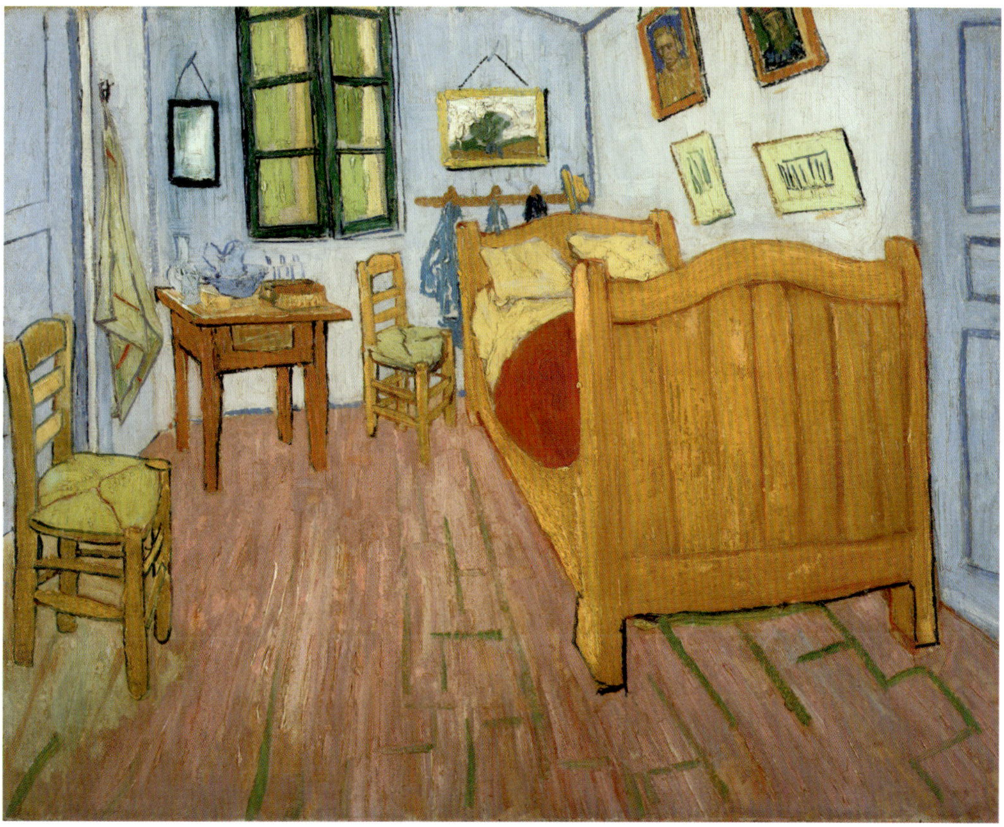

44
Vincent van Gogh
Portrait of Paul Gauguin, 1888
Van Gogh Museum, Amsterdam

45
Paul Gauguin
The little cat, 1888
Private collection

46
Vincent van Gogh
Sunflowers, 1888
Seiji Togo Memorial Sompo Japan Museum of Art, Tokyo

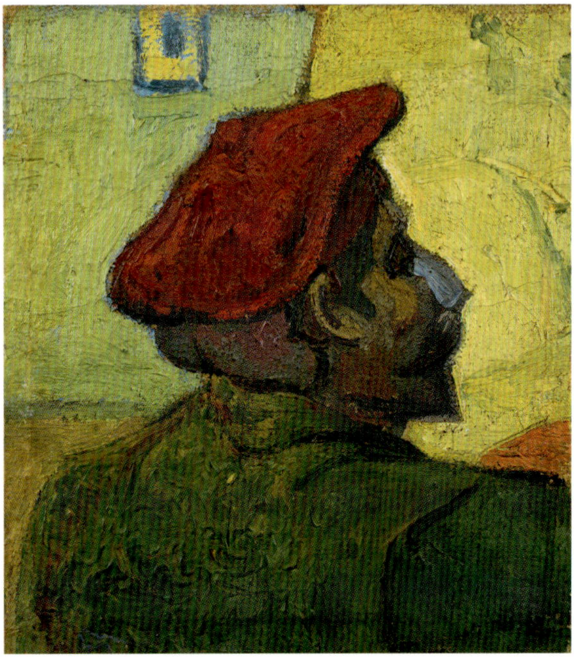

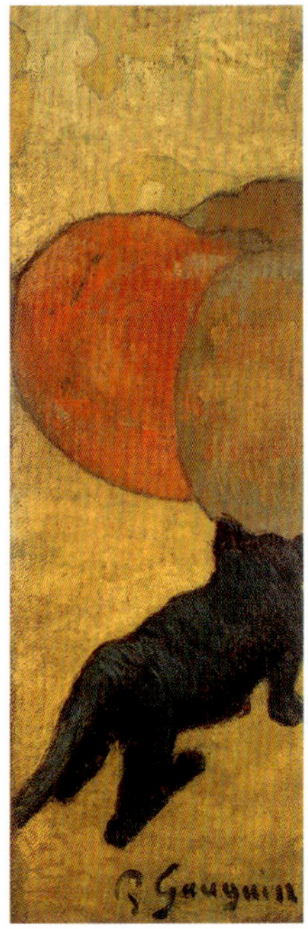

At the same time, Van Gogh made a free repetition of his last still life of sunflowers (37), in which he made the forms even more schematic and sought a better solution for the light-on-light effect (46). The original has a light yellow background with a barely perceptible greenish yellow on top, but in the new version he used not the yellow but a saturated form of the greenish yellow. The work was also painted on a new kind of support, coarse jute, which Gauguin had bought for both of them after his arrival, and it forced Van Gogh to find new ways of using his varied brush-strokes. For example, if he wanted to prevent the texture of the jute from influencing the final result he could not repeat the thinly painted passages in the vase and the foreground without running into problems. He was therefore forced to paint them thickly, making them even more pronounced and impasted than elsewhere in the picture. He then echoed the impasto in the petals.

This artistic dialogue between Van Gogh and Gauguin in the form of

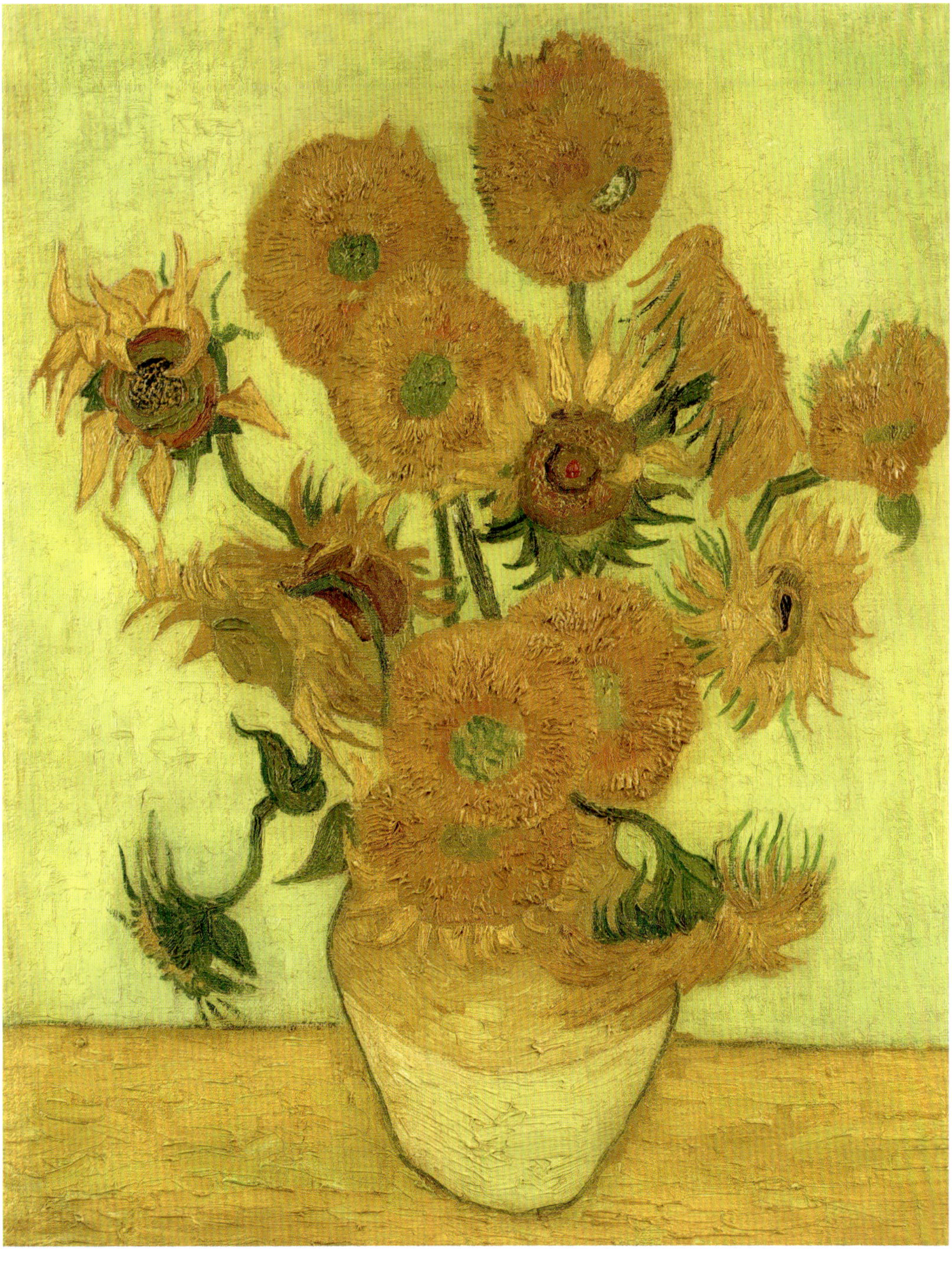

47
Paul Gauguin
Vincent van Gogh painting sunflowers, 1888
Van Gogh Museum, Amsterdam

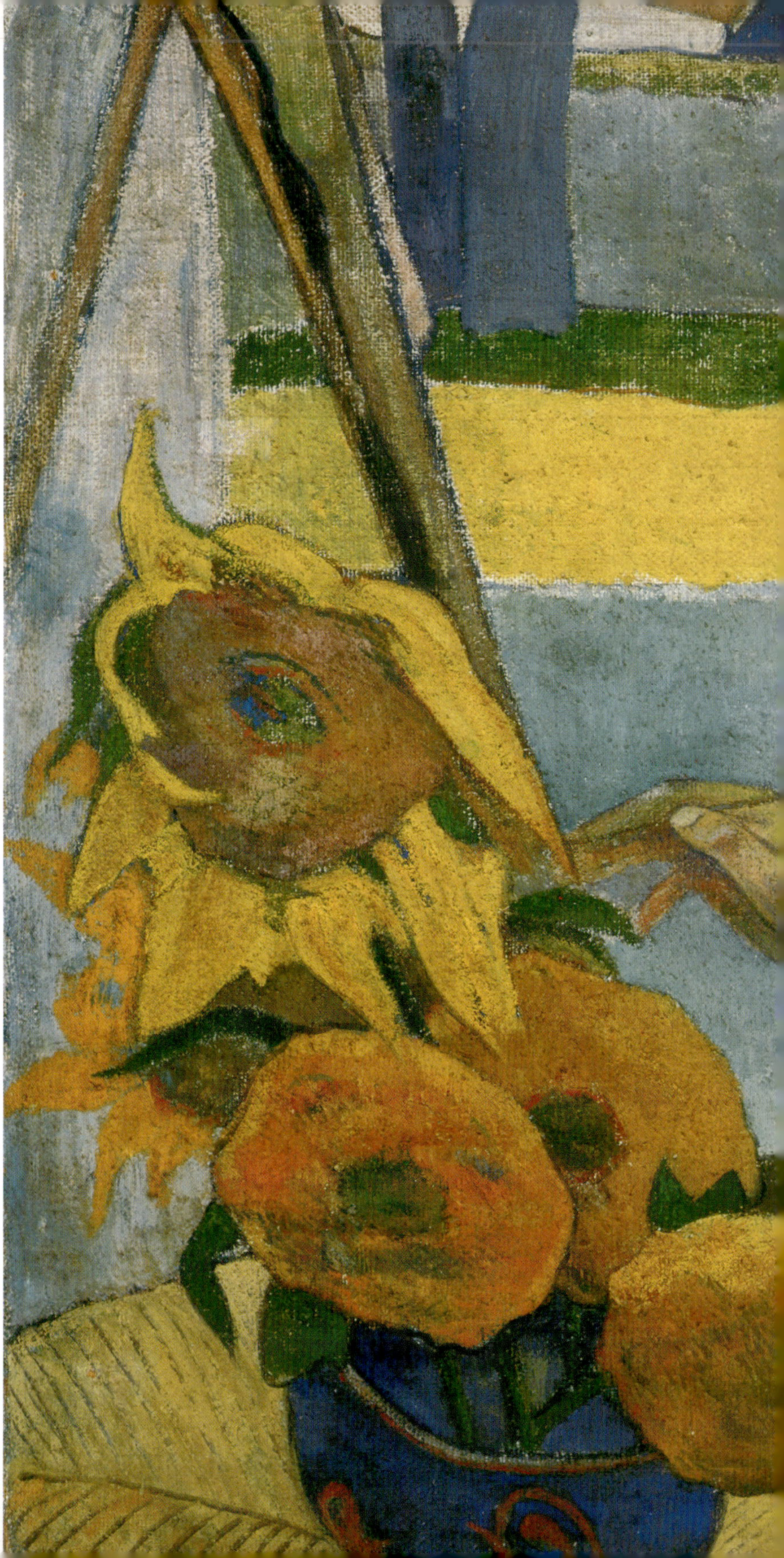

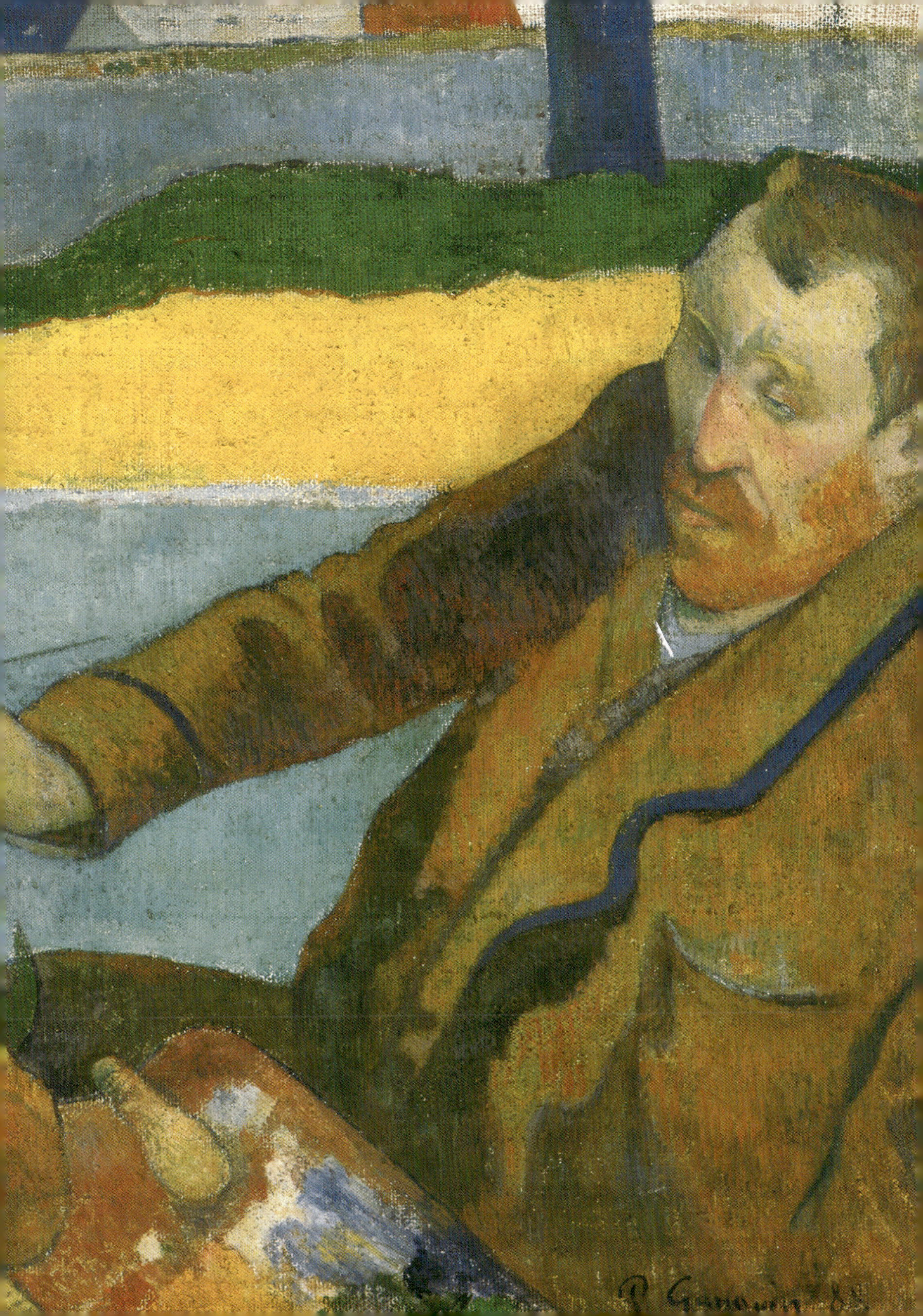

two still lifes was parallelled in the portraits they painted of each other at almost the same time. Van Gogh showed his companion at work in front of a yellow painting, which, given the spherical object on the left, must be the still life with a pumpkin (44). Gauguin, in turn, depicted Van Gogh painting a still life with sunflowers (47), but it is not at all true to life. He is shown with a vase of the flowers on the table in front of him, which was an invention on Gauguin's part, for Van Gogh had painted his recent still life on the basis of the version he had completed in August, and in October the sunflowers had long since finished flowering.

In essence, Gauguin portrayed his colleague as a realist, as someone who always needed to work from life. Van Gogh did not find this image of himself inaccurate, not even in the case of *Sunflowers*, but the irony is that at this very time he was trying to follow Gauguin's example by being as abstract as possible and work from the imagination. He did so in his portrait of Gauguin, but, as Gauguin had immortalized him as the kind of artist he did not want to be, one wonders whether he was really happy with the result.

TRIPTYCH

The collaboration between the two artists came to an abrupt end in December 1888 when Van Gogh cut off part of his ear in a fit of madness, the first sign of his illness, which was probably a form of epilepsy. Gauguin then left Arles. He had wanted to go earlier, but after this incident he would not stay a moment longer. Van Gogh was admitted to hospital, and later complained to Theo about 'the queer phenomenon of Gauguin's behaviour in choosing not to speak to me again and clearing out'.

When Van Gogh had recovered a little he asked his friend 'to refrain ... from speaking ill of our poor little yellow house'. We only know some of Gauguin's reply, because much of his letter has been lost. In exchange for a few studies he had left behind, or as an outright gift, he asked for the yellow still life with sunflowers, which he rightly regarded as 'a perfect example of a style that is completely Vincent's'. We know that he was

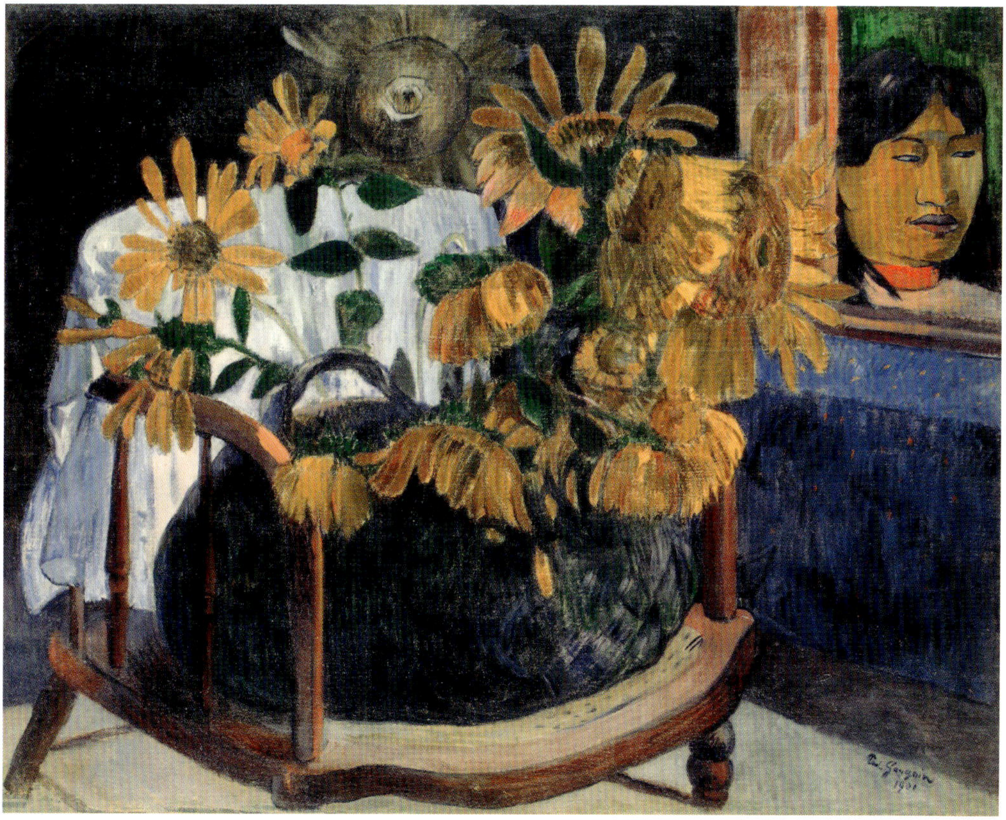

48
Paul Gauguin
Sunflowers on an armchair, 1901
The State Hermitage Museum, St Petersburg

also intrigued by the unrealistic green hearts of the large sunflowers that were going to seed (36, 37), for he later described them as ‘flowers of the sun, with ... eyes’, and painted a sunflower in the same way himself (48), giving an interpretation that was all his own to Van Gogh’s schematic, primitive form.

Vincent wrote grumpily to Theo about Gauguin’s proposal, which had probably been made rather bluntly and unceremoniously. ‘I think it rather strange,’ he wrote, ‘that he claims a picture of sunflowers from me.’ Vincent definitely wanted to keep his sunflower pictures. After all, his friend had ‘two of them already, let that be enough for him’. Addressing Gauguin himself, however, Van Gogh took a more conciliatory tone. On the one hand he was angry about his departure, but on the other hand

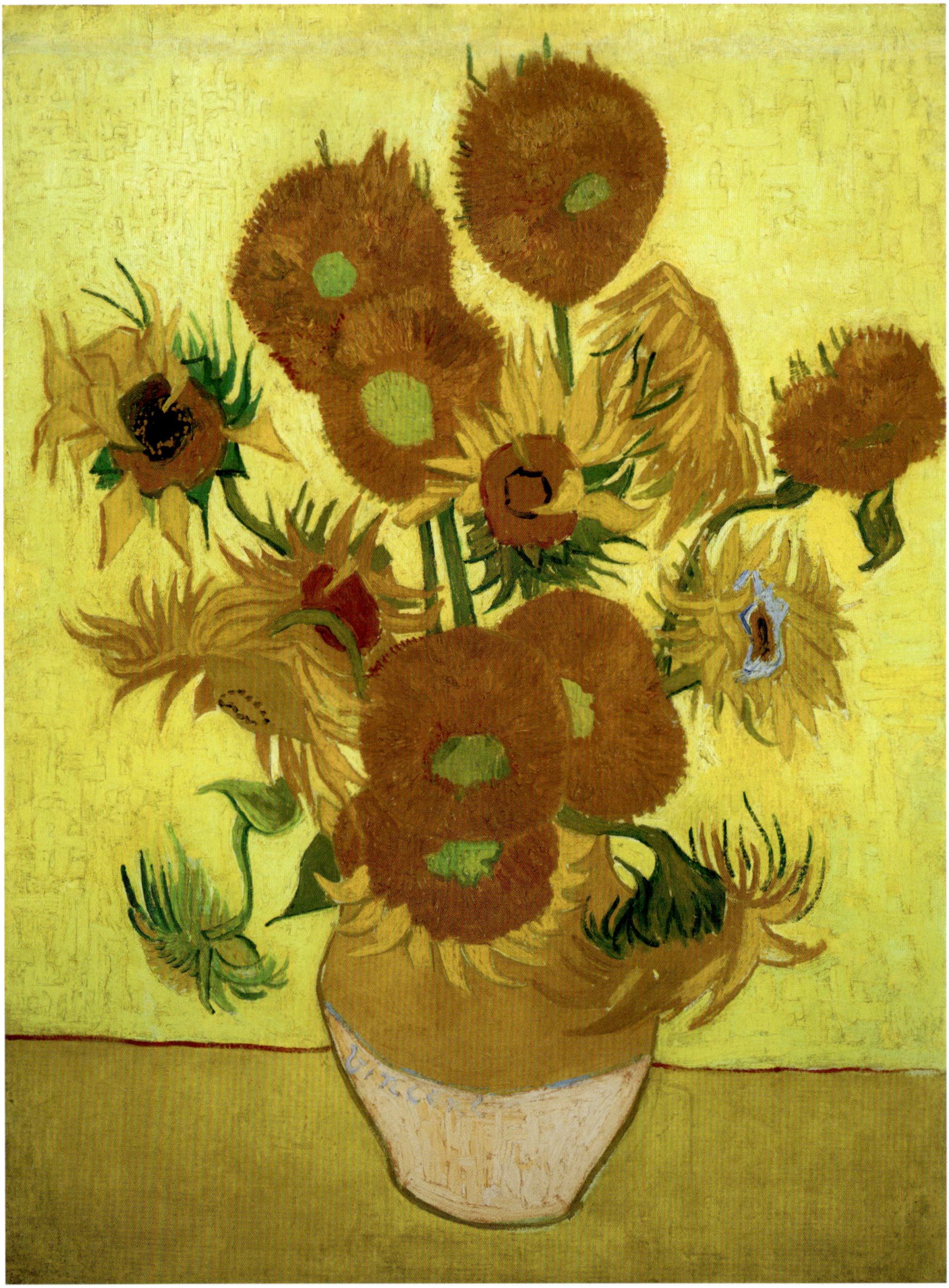

49 Vincent van Gogh, *Sunflowers*, 1889, Van Gogh Museum, Amsterdam

he wanted to make his excuses to his colleague as if he needed to make up with him. His desire to conciliate gained the upper hand, partly because he was still hoping that they could resume their collaboration. 'You speak of a canvas of mine in your letter, the sunflowers against a yellow background, to make it clear that you would like to have it. I don't think you've made a bad choice: if Jeannin has the peony, Quost the hollyhock, then I indeed have taken the sunflower before others.' But, he added, allowing a little of his anger to show through, he categorically contested Gauguin's 'right to the canvas in question'. He then ended on a more diplomatic note, saying that he would nevertheless grant Gauguin's request, but in another way. He would make a new version, and do his best to 'make it exactly the same'.

However, Van Gogh then went and did something different. He made repetitions of both of the still lifes in the guest room, and went to great lengths to make them a matching pair, as far as possible; as a result they are certainly not exactly the same as the originals (49, 51). He made the shapes of the flowers even more schematic, changed the colour of the bottom half of the vase into a purplish tone, and put in new colour accents, among them blue and orange. He painted the background the same colour as his very last variant (46) – greenish yellow rather than yellow. In his repetition of the original with the yellow background from the summer of 1888 (49), he even heightened the interplay between impasted and flat passages. He made the thin foreground contrast with the thicker part of the bottom half of the vase, but now painted the top half thinly, like the petals.

This repetition of the two still lifes was a result of his recent completion of *La Berceuse* (50). He had started on this portrait of Augustine Roulin as a mother rocking a cradle in the last weeks of Gauguin's stay in Arles, but now he came up with the idea of two triptychs, with *La Berceuse* in the middle and *Sunflowers* on either side. He thought that the yellow still life (49) should go on the left and the blue one (51) on the right, as can be seen from a sketch in one his later letters (52). One triptych would be for Theo,

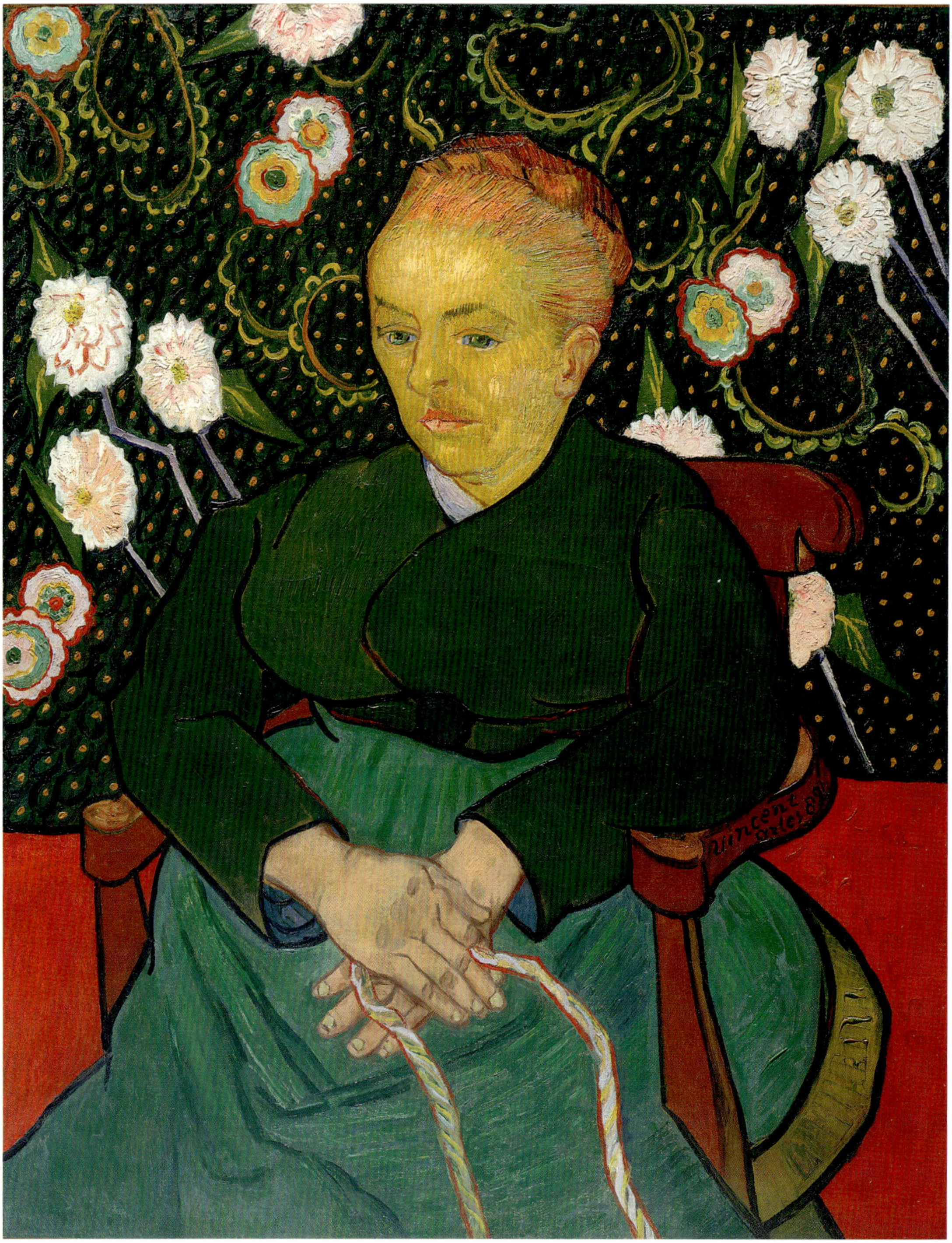

50 Vincent van Gogh, *La Berceuse* (Woman rocking a cradle), 1889, The Metropolitan Museum of Art, New York

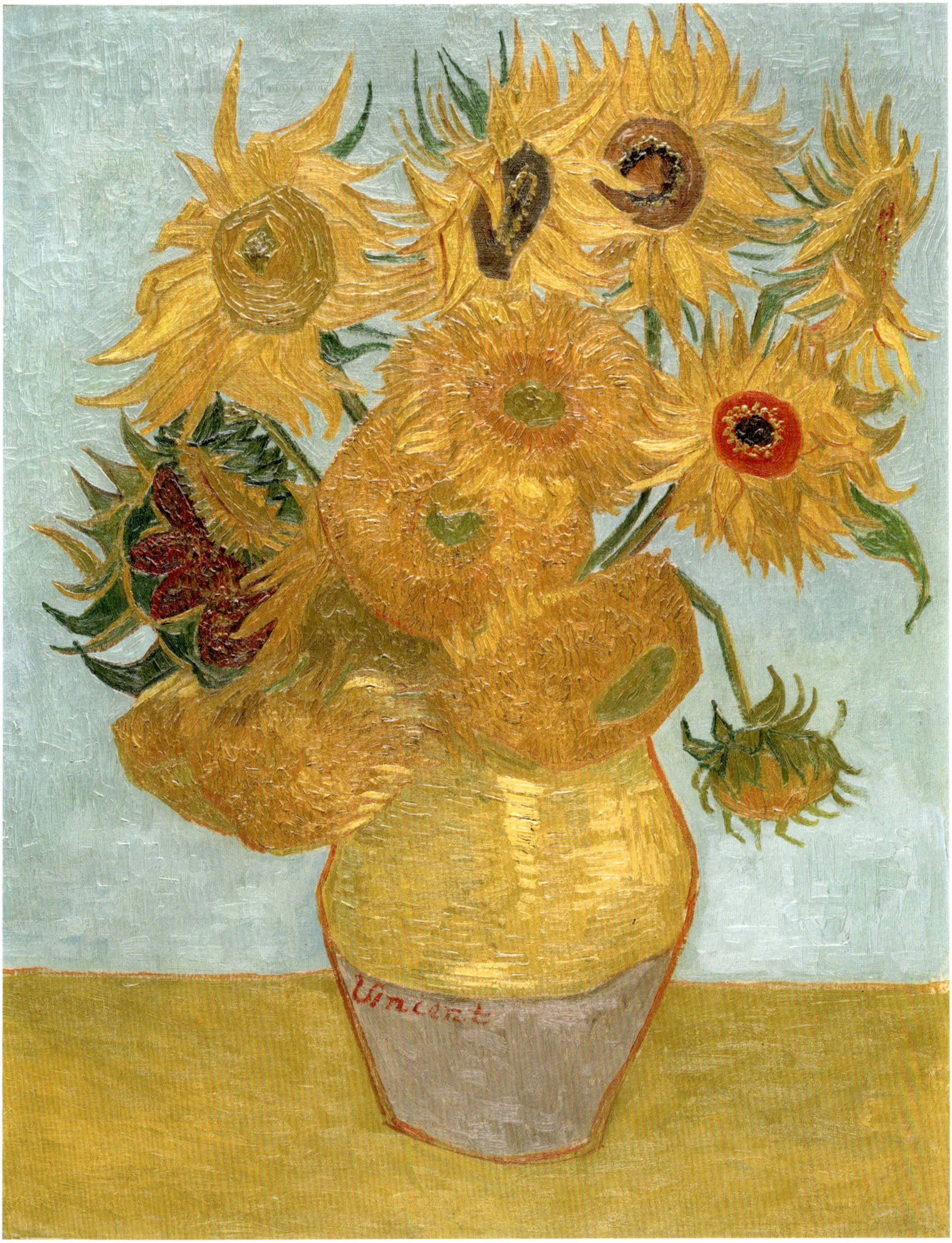

51 Vincent van Gogh, *Sunflowers*, 1889, Philadelphia Museum of Art

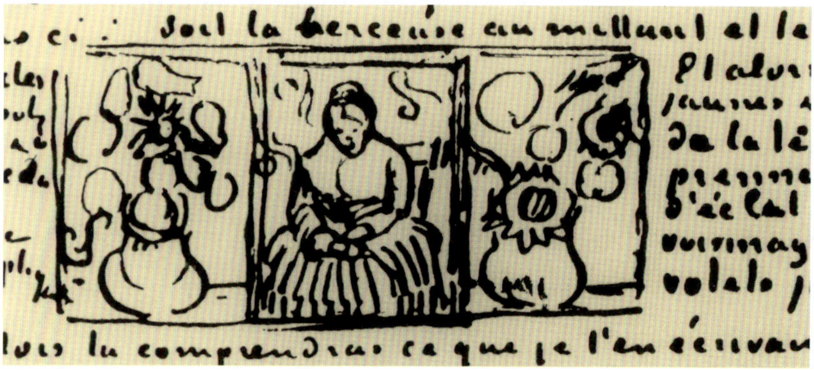

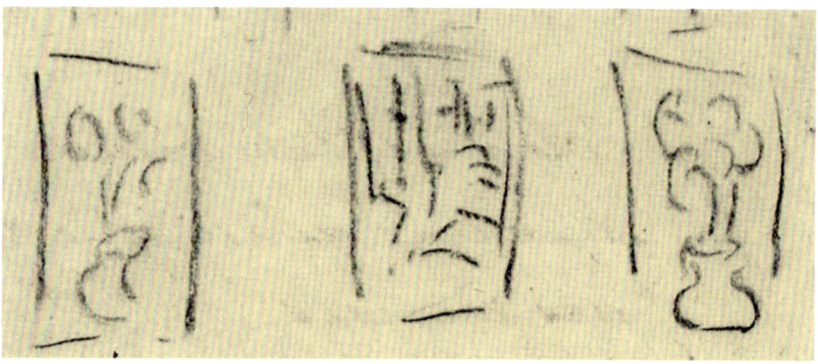

52 Vincent van Gogh, Sketch in a letter to Theo van Gogh, 22 May 1889, present whereabouts unknown
53 Vincent van Gogh, Sketch in a letter to Octave Maus, 15 November 1889, Van Gogh Museum, Amsterdam

the other for Gauguin. The latter knew nothing of this, but Van Gogh assumed that his colleague would be prepared to make an exchange, for the triptych would include a repetition of the still life with the yellow background that he had asked for.

Van Gogh did his very best to present that triptych as a coherent entity. The seated woman with the cord attached to the cradle is shown in the evening, so he conceived of his yellow still lifes as 'standard lamps or candelabra'. Van Gogh portrait of Augustine Roulin was intended to be a mark of homage to motherhood in general, so he gave the still lifes a meaning that was in keeping with that. He later wrote, at least, that they 'express an idea symbolizing "gratitude"', and this can only be understood in the context of their function as the wings flanking *La Berceuse*.

Van Gogh's tacit decision to send Gauguin a triptych instead of a simple repetition of the sunflower still life he had asked for was probably due to his dissatisfaction with his friend's choice. It dated from before the time when they had worked together, and from this he must have deduced that Gauguin did not have a very high opinion of what he had been painting when they were together. That was painful, certainly in the light of his hope for a renewed collaboration. Moreover, he did not consider the flower still lifes to be the most important things he had done recently. True, they were a great achievement and certainly worth a lot of money, but when he returned from hospital at the beginning of 1889 he declared that the best of his paintings was the *Bedroom* (43), which he had painted a few weeks after the *Sunflowers*.

However, after he finished *La Berceuse* he felt that it put all his previous work in the shade. 'As an Impressionist arrangement of colours, I've never devised anything better', he wrote. Unlike the *Sunflowers*, he had not painted it directly from life but had put it together in the studio using studies. The canvas was an 'abstraction', and as such the crowning achievement of the learning process he had recently gone through, when he tried to follow Gauguin's example by working from the imagination. If he was to be represented in his friend's collection with a recent work in order to underline the value of their collaboration, then this was it. In the meantime Gauguin had only asked for the *Sunflowers* with the yellow background, but by creating a triptych he cleverly did justice to his own high opinion of *La Berceuse* while at the same time acceding to his friend's request. Van Gogh probably regarded both works as the best things that he had ever produced in the way of 'comforting' art, and that was another very legitimate reason for combining them.

At the beginning of May he sent his paintings from Arles to Theo in Paris, telling him that he could now present Gauguin with 'the copy of *La Berceuse*'. He said nothing more about the triptych, and if Gauguin wanted the *Sunflowers*, which Van Gogh still assumed he did, 'it is only fair that he should give you something you like equally well in return'. Theo did as Vincent asked, and in the summer Gauguin, who was back in Brittany by then, let him know that he accepted the painting. However, he said nothing about an exchange, and asked Theo to hold on to *La Berceuse* for him.

Interestingly enough, Van Gogh started thinking differently about *La Berceuse* when he was in the asylum in Saint-Rémy. He now felt that this kind of abstracted art was beyond his capabilities, and he called the painting 'a failure and ... feeble'. When, in late 1889, he was invited to take part in the annual exhibition of the Les Vingt artists' society in Brussels he accordingly left this portrait out of the selection, but did include the two still lifes with sunflowers, which Theo had also praised. It is known from a surviving sketch (53) that he wanted them to hang on either side of the *Trees with ivy* (54) that he had painted in Saint-Rémy, which he would have regarded as a good substitute for the unloved *Berceuse* because it contained a lot of green.

Perhaps strengthened by the friendly words of the influential critic Albert Aurier in early 1890, Van Gogh then turned to flower pieces once again, although with fewer pretensions than before. Prior to his departure for Auvers-sur-Oise, when the flowering season had only just begun, he painted four related still lifes, one of which, *Irises* (56), can be seen as

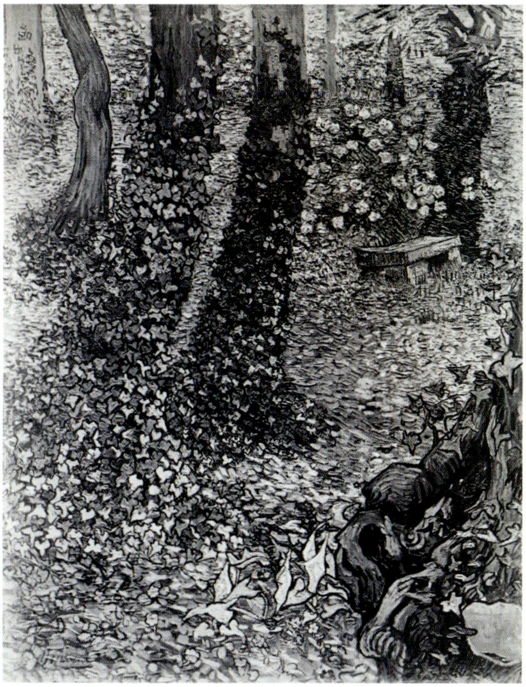

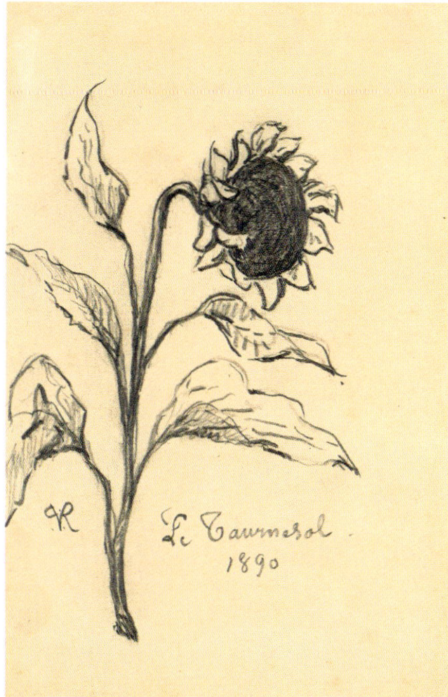

54
Vincent van Gogh
Trees with ivy, 1889
Lost in the Second World War

55
Paul Gachet Sr
Sunflower, 1890
Van Gogh Museum, Amsterdam

the pictorial continuation of his exercise in blues and yellows that he had begun with the sunflowers. When he started planning a series of etchings of Provençal subjects in Auvers, he thought of including that work together with his two sunflower still lifes from Arles, as emerges from his sketchbook, in which he drew the three of them from memory (57, 58). He painted other flower still lifes in his new home, but with two exceptions they were only small studies. He no longer had high ambitions.

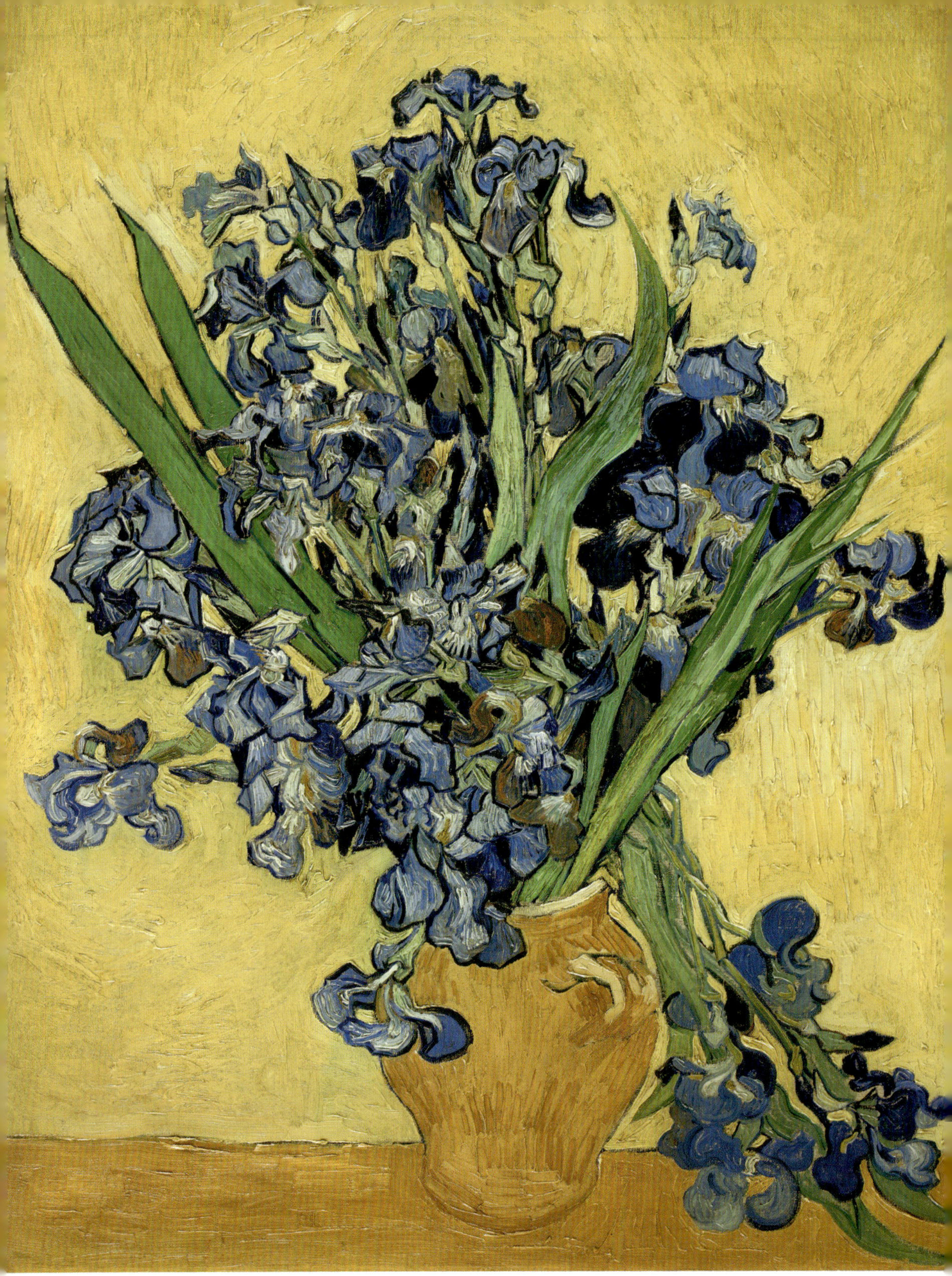

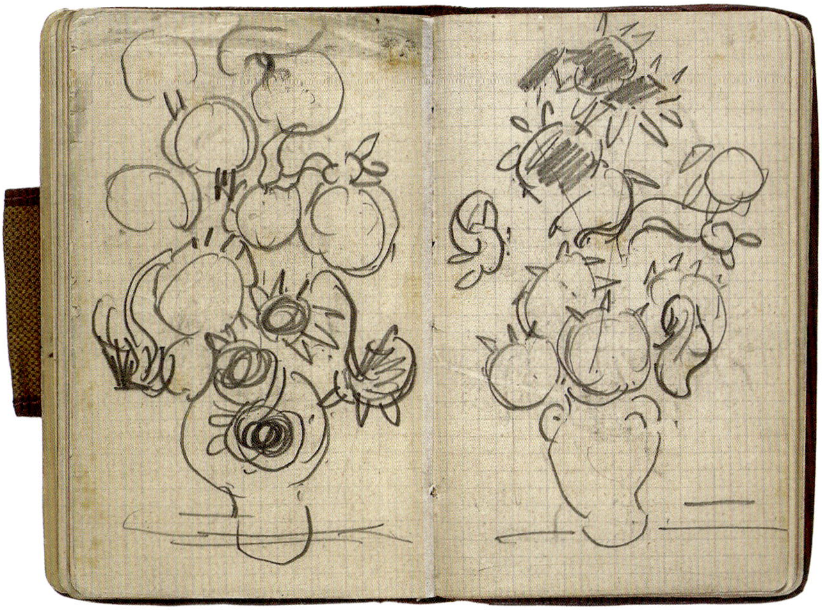

56
Vincent van Gogh
Irises, 1890
Van Gogh Museum,
Amsterdam

57
Vincent van Gogh
Sketches of vases with
sunflowers, 1890
Van Gogh Museum,
Amsterdam

58
Vincent van Gogh
Sketch of a vase
of irises, 1890
Van Gogh Museum,
Amsterdam

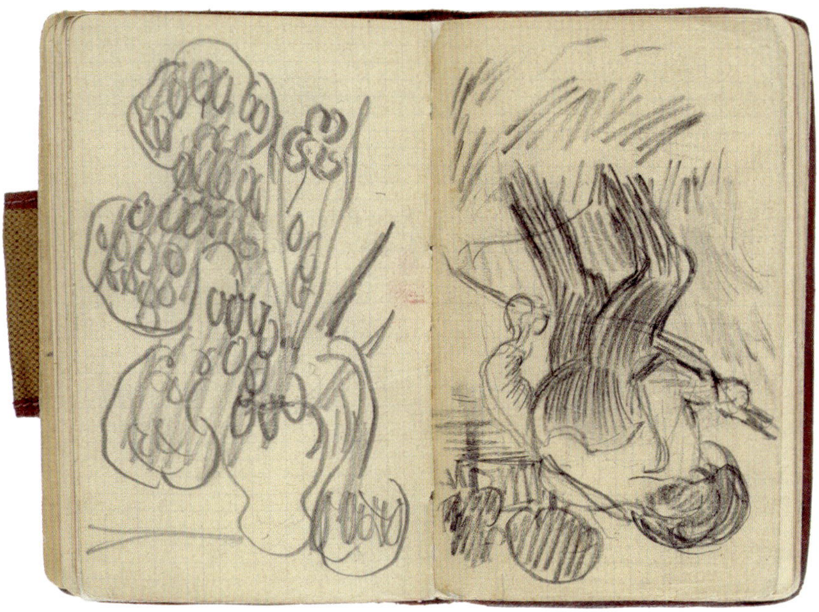

REPUTATION AND INTERPRETATION

Van Gogh shot himself in the chest on 27 July 1890 and died two days later. The funeral took place the following day, and Paul Gachet, the doctor who had been looking after Vincent, was the first to arrive, bringing 'a magnificent bunch of sunflowers because he loved them so much', as Theo wrote to his wife Jo. In the end there were not only sunflowers on the bier, but also 'yellow dahlias, yellow flowers everywhere'. Gachet almost immediately sowed sunflowers on the grave, and later made a drawing of them growing there, which he sent to the inconsolable Theo (55).

Shortly after Van Gogh's death, critics took a great interest in his achievements as a flower painter. The Dutch critic Johan de Meester wrote: 'It was in his flower paintings, I believe, that Van Gogh was the purest, the most singular, painter. When he executed landscapes, the thinker, the poet, the Symbolist was too easily awakened in him, but with flowers he often succeeded in limiting himself to their charm and to bringing to life on canvas the splendour of their colours.' The Danish painter Johan Rohde felt the same in 1892: 'Van Gogh's talent has unfolded most simply and most beautifully in some unassuming pictures of flowers'.

Although people also liked Van Gogh's *Irises*, the greatest praise was reserved for the large still lifes of sunflowers painted in Arles. 'I find this a wonderful work', observed the Dutch art teacher Hendrik Bremmer in 1911 about the painting with the blue background (36). 'Superb, because it ... far exceeds *our* insight into such a piece of reality.' The critic Charles John Holmes was equally enthusiastic in 1910 about the still life that is now in Tokyo (46). It was 'a magnificent decorative panel', in which he particularly valued the fact that Van Gogh's search for a certain abstraction in colour and form had not been made at the expense of faithfulness to the flowers themselves: 'When we come to examine it closely, we discover that these great sunflowers seem to be alive, their petals seem to writhe and flicker like flames, their hearts to be quivering with intense unearthly fire. I know no other painting of such uncanny attractiveness.' The reputation of Sunflowers was so great that imitations were soon

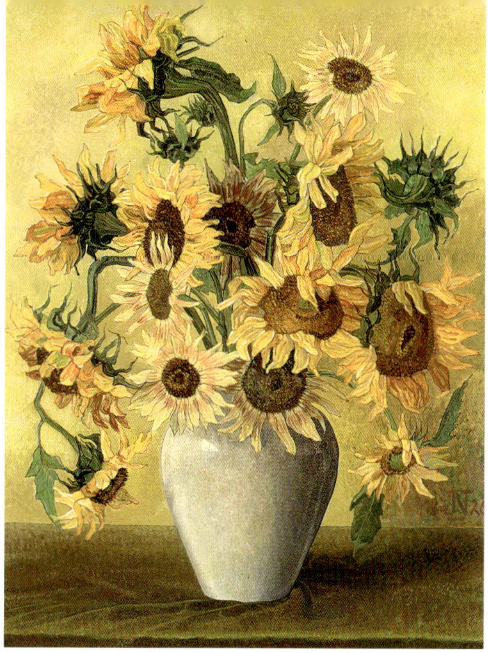

59
Jacob (Jaap) Nieweg
Sunflowers, 1926
Galerie Dolf D. van Omme, Amsterdam

being made, though some artists stayed closer to the original (59) than others (60).

When Van Gogh died, all the still lifes of sunflowers were still in Theo's collection, apart from the two from the Paris period that had been given to Gauguin (18, 20). However, they were soon dispersed. Seven of the nine in the collection of Theo's widow Jo van Gogh-Bonger found their way to dealers, influential collectors and museums. In 1908 Helene Kröller-Müller, who was to install her collection in the museum in Otterlo that bears her name, bought Van Gogh's large still life of sunflowers from the Paris period (21), making it one of the very first, if not the very first, work by Van Gogh in her collection. Hugo von Tschudi, the director of the Nationalgalerie in Berlin, bought the still life with the blue background for his own collection in 1905 (36). In 1912, that and other Van Goghs from his collection were acquired by the Neue Pinakothek in Munich, where Tschudi had been appointed director three years previously. This was an important museum for a modern artist, and that was one of the reasons why Jo van Gogh-Bonger gave in when Charles Aitken, the director of the Tate Gallery, London's modern art museum, asked her in 1924 to sell the still life from the family collection that Gauguin had so much wanted to have (37). 'For two days I have tried to harden my heart against your

60

Egon Schiele

Autumn sun, 1914

Private collection

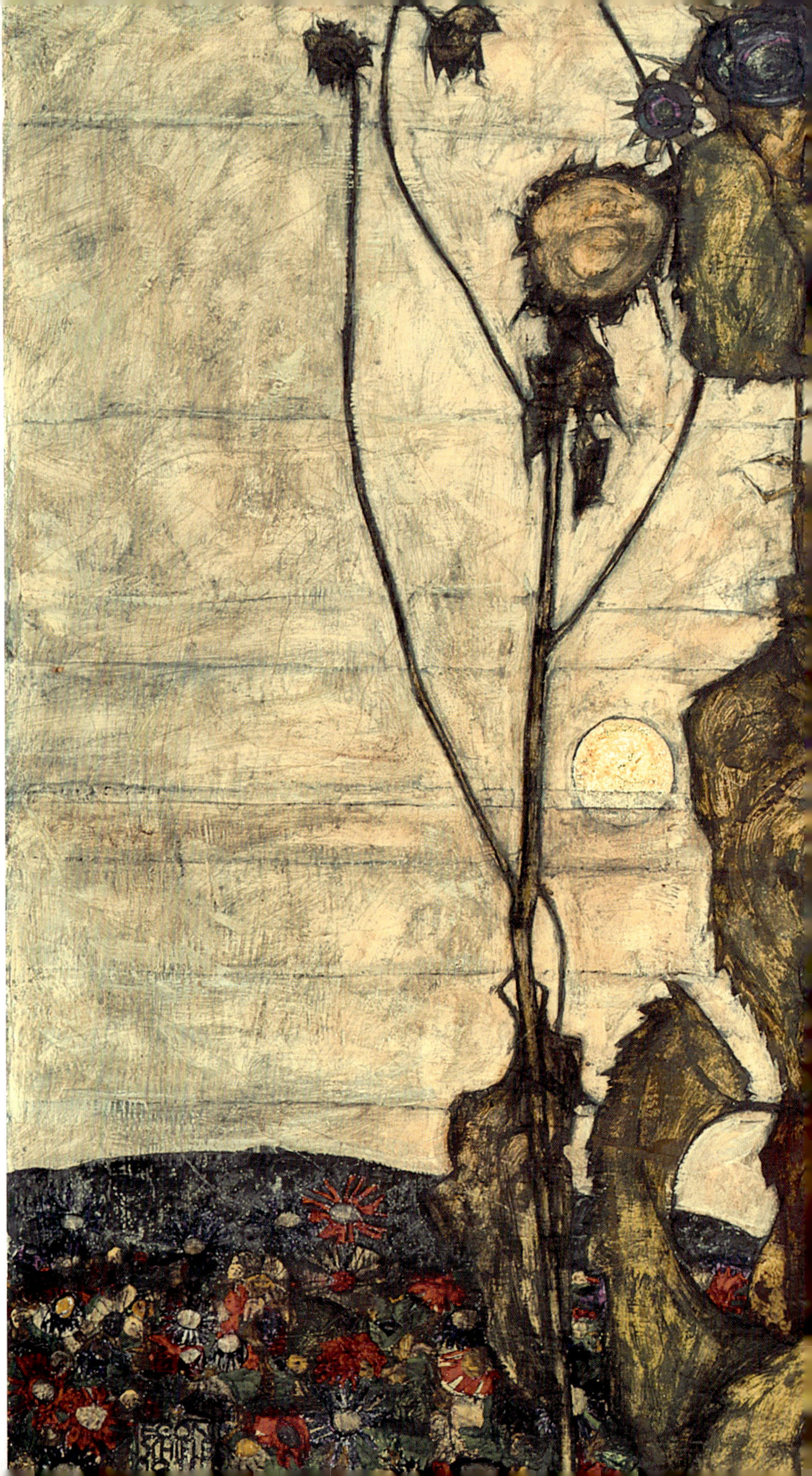

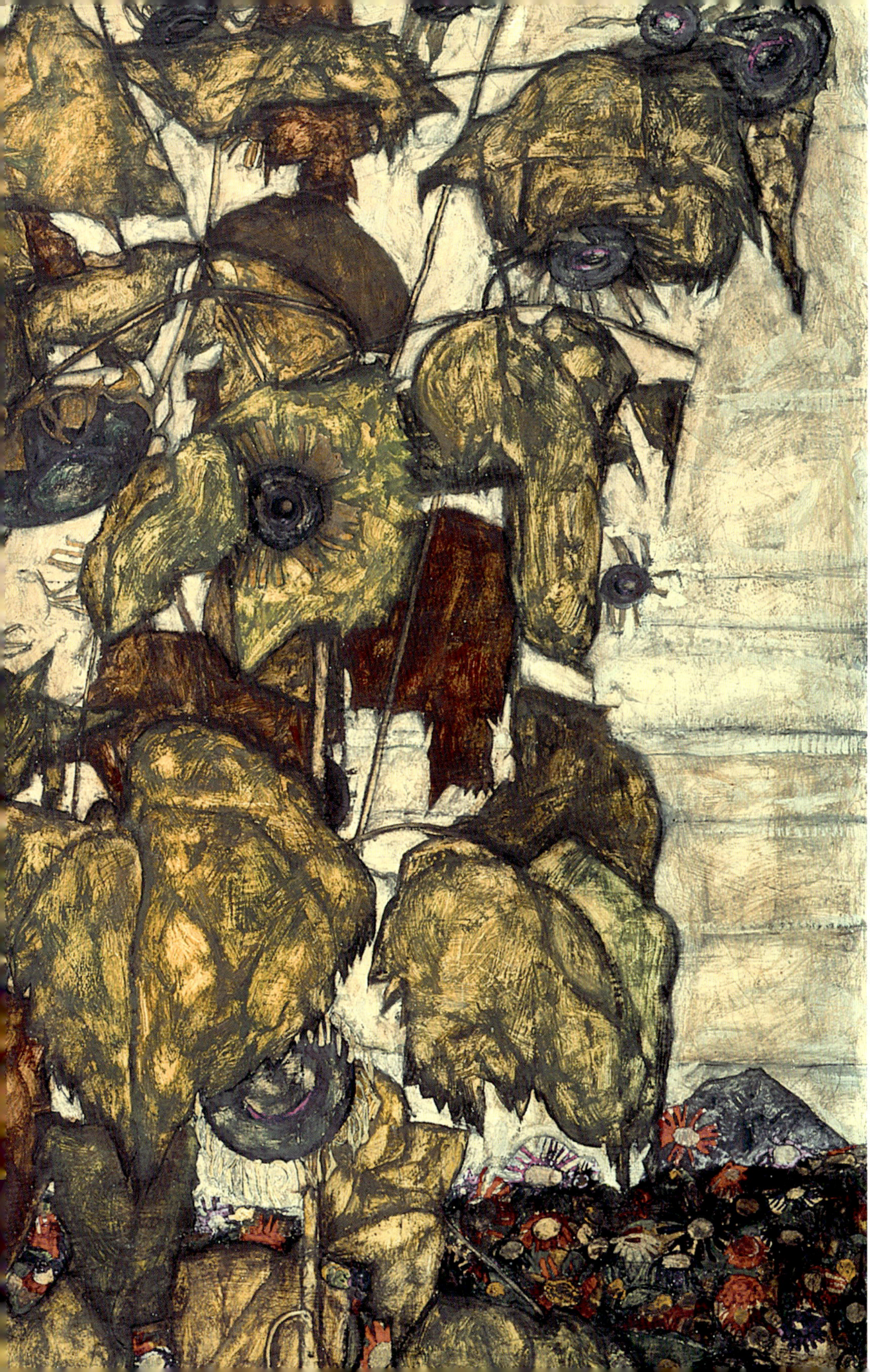

appeal', she wrote to Aitken. 'I felt as if I could not bear to separate from the picture I have looked on every day for more than thirty years. But at the end the appeal proved irresistible. I know that no picture would represent Vincent in your famous Gallery in a more worthy manner than the "Sunflowers", and that he himself, "le Peintre des Tournesols", would have liked it to be there. So I am willing to ... leave you the "Sunflowers" at the price noted for the insurance. It is a sacrifice for the sake of Vincent's glory.'

The financial value of the sunflower still lifes was by now going up by leaps and bounds. Tschudi paid 3,200 German marks for his, Helene Kröller-Müller paid 4,800 guilders, and Aitken 15,000 guilders – all of them top prices for a Van Gogh at the time. The absolute pinnacle was reached in 1988, when the repetition of the 1888 yellow still life (46) was bought by the Japanese insurance company Yasuda Fire & Marine Insurance for £24.75 million. That was then the world record for any painting, and many people believed that it would make it impossible to view the picture with an unprejudiced eye. The conceptual artist Rose Finn-Kelcey wittily commented on the criticism and excitement by replicating the still life with coins painted gold, silver and copper, with viewers being allowed to see the work in the gallery from a platform under the watchful eye of real security guards (61).

But money is money and art is art, and the painting itself has not been altered by the high price paid for it. It is true that it is difficult to look at it with an open mind, but that is more because of the authoritative interpretations of the *Sunflowers* that were aired after Van Gogh's death. Associations were made at an early stage with the symbolism of the sunflower, which has a respectable and rich tradition. It is said to turn its head to follow the sun, and although that is not strictly true (it only does so until it starts flowering) this natural phenomenon meant that it was associated not only with the sun but also with love – initially only the love of God but later of mankind and the supernatural as well.

All of this was projected on to the still lifes of sunflowers. When the critic Albert Aurier referred to Van Gogh's *Sunflowers* in 1890, he wondered 'how could we explain that obsessive passion for the solar disk ... if we refuse to accept his persistent preoccupation with some vague and glorious heliomythic allegory?' The fact is that many people thought that Van Gogh was indeed searching for sunshine and light in his work, and that this quest must have been depicted in the still lifes in some way or other. Van Gogh thus became a sunflower himself, and that is how Richard Roland Holst rendered him in 1892 (62), but in the form of a sacred sunflower by adding a halo. It indicated that Van Gogh's own 'turning' towards the light and the sun had come to an end: the head has finished flowering and the sun is setting. This image of the artist was still so topical 23 years later that the artist Huszár presented it in the same way in his painting *Vincent*, but did so in another formal vocabulary, that of Futurism (63).

61
Rose Finn-Kelcey
Bureau de change, 1988
Performance in the
Matts Gallery, London

However, there is not the slightest indication that Van Gogh ever regarded the plant as symbolizing his persona as an artist, or interpreted

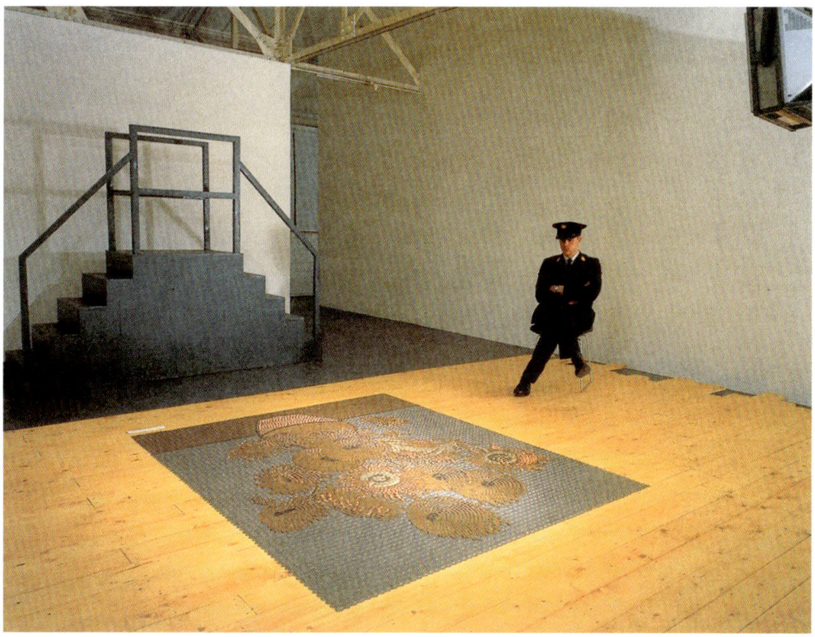

62
Richard N. Roland Holst
Cover of the catalogue of the Van Gogh exhibition in the Panorama Gebouw, Amsterdam, 1892
Van Gogh Museum Library, Amsterdam

63
Vilmor Herz (Huszár)
Vincent, 1915
Private collection

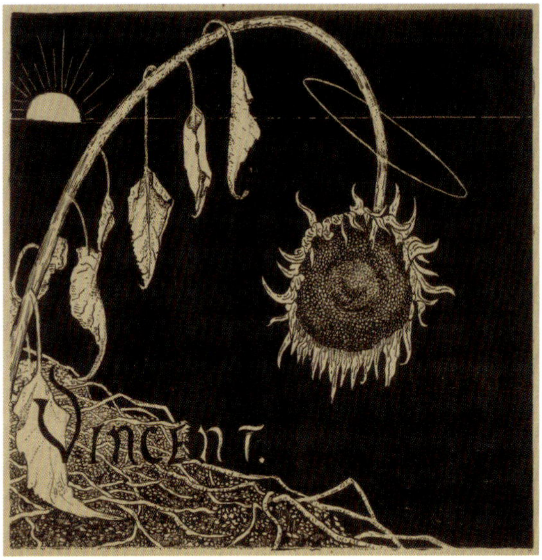

it as a mysterious metaphor of love and the supernatural. Nor did he want his *Sunflowers* to symbolize sunny Provence, as has been suggested. The colourful surroundings there stimulated him in his search for bold yellows, but that does not mean that that colour represented the region. Nor did the sunflower itself. Waving fields of the flower are nowadays typical of Provence, but they did not yet exist in Van Gogh's day, despite what people often think – as so wittily summed up in a cartoon by Gerhard Glück (65). In the nineteenth century there were only fields of lavender there, and he painted them – but only once (64).

Van Gogh's *Sunflowers* do carry a loftier message, but it lies in the *depiction* of the plants. The flowers are everyday, rather humble blooms as it were, and have resigned themselves to their fate by flowering and withering. For Van Gogh, that gave them a human or, if one likes, religious significance. This brought comfort, and that is what he wanted to evoke with his scintillating colours.

This message is no longer seen in the *Sunflowers*, so their present popularity is due more to the successful form of the composition, and above all to the bold yellows. Although the colours have darkened a little, the

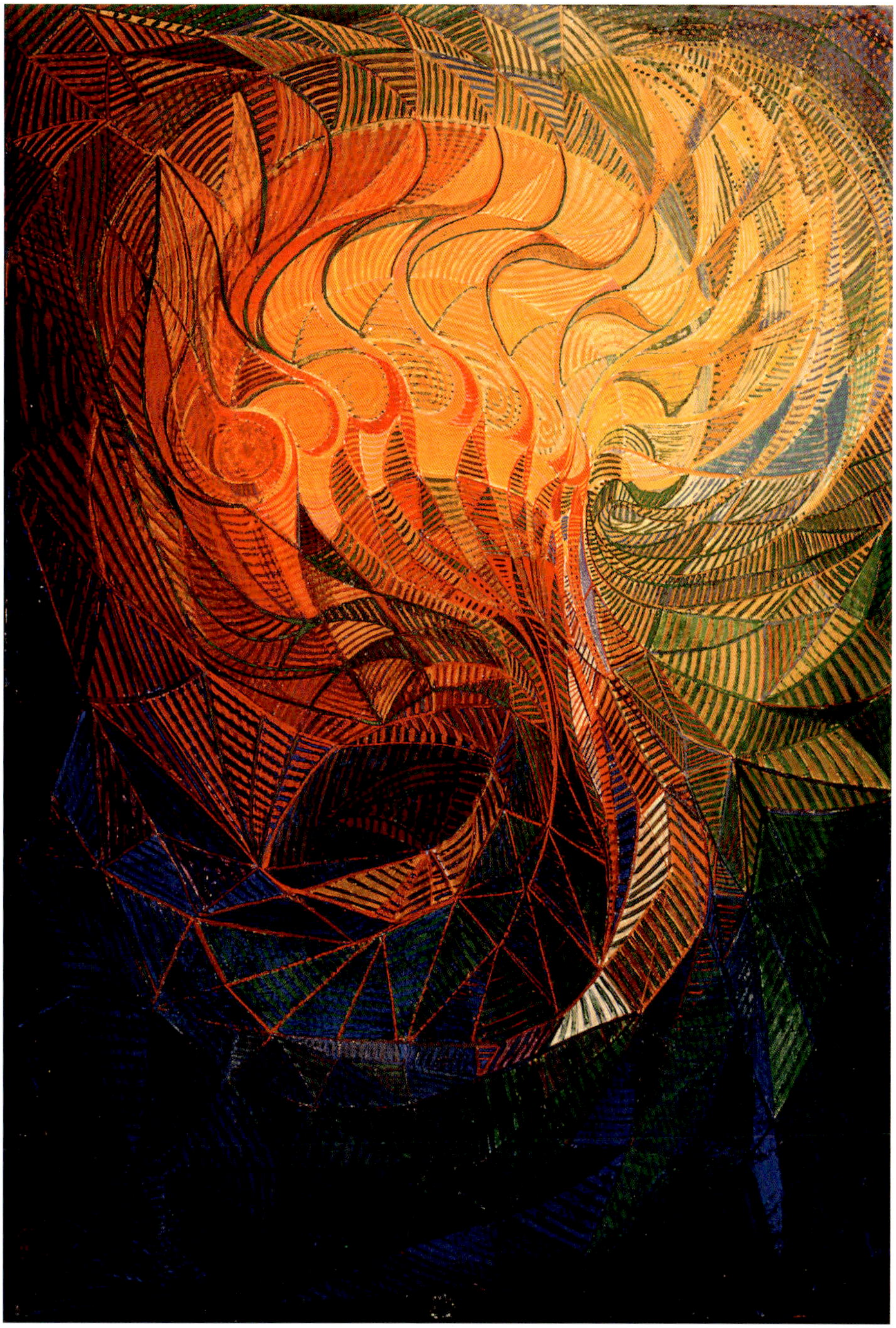

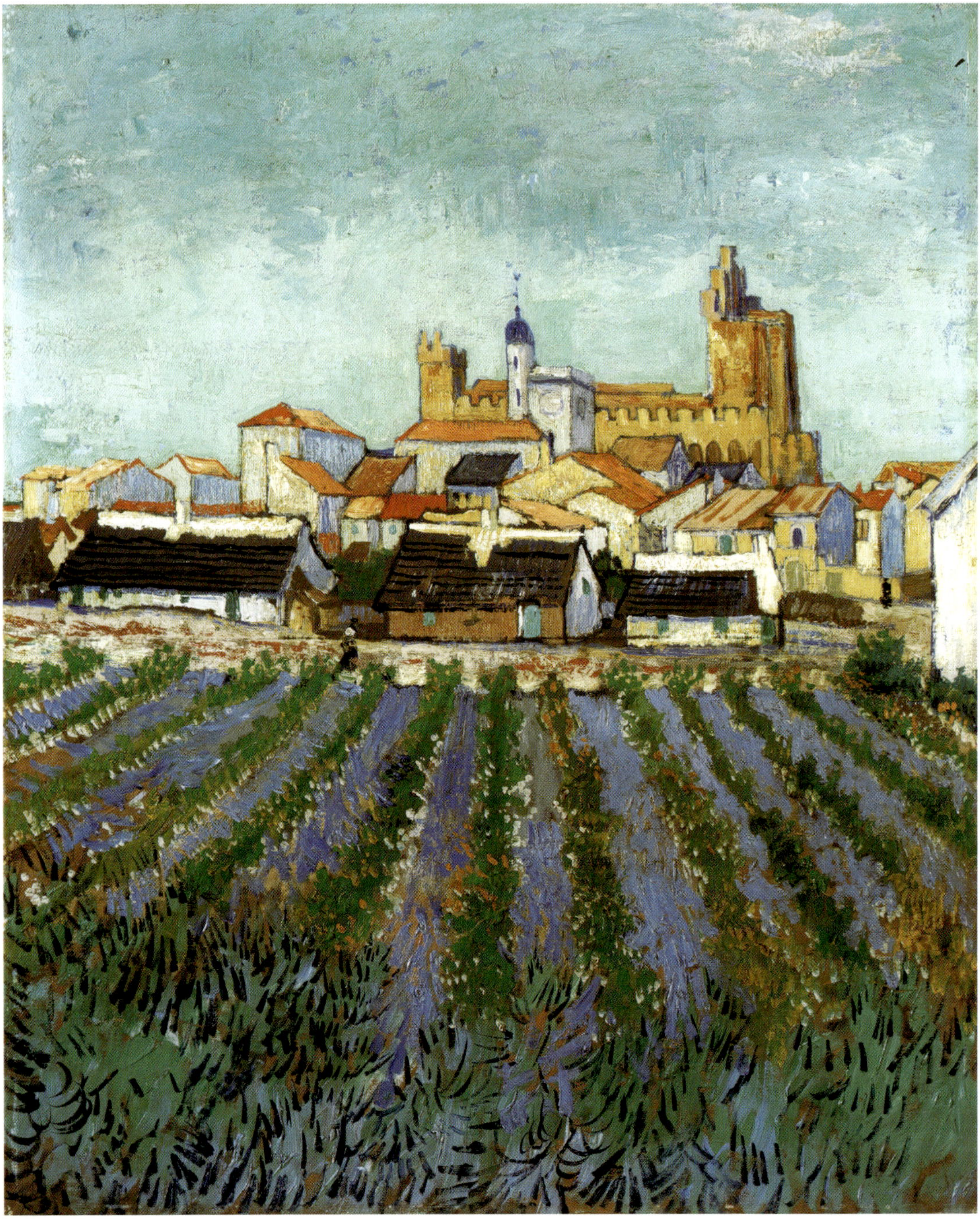

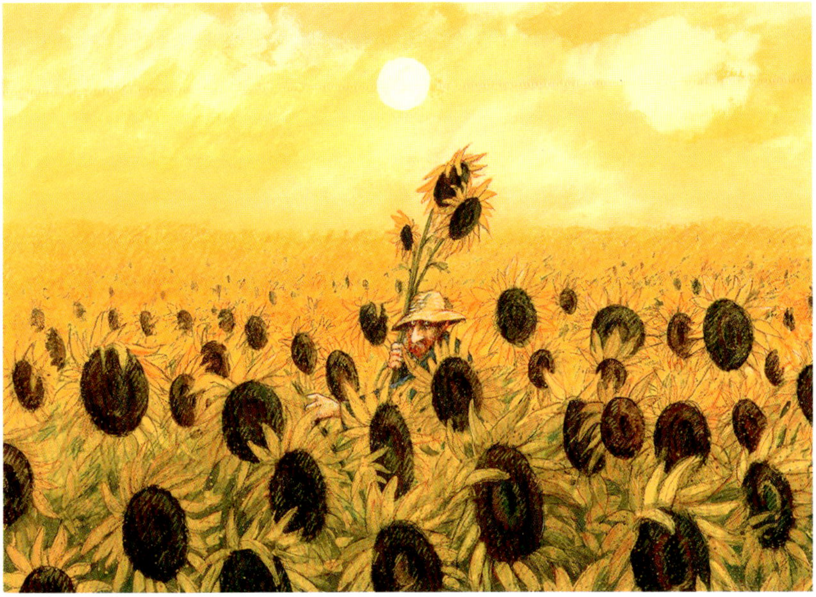

64
Vincent van Gogh
View of Les Saintes-Maries-de-la-Mer, 1888
Kröller-Müller Museum, Otterlo

65
Gerhard Glück
Vincent pinching sunflowers again, 1990

still life is still more radiant than any other painting in Van Gogh's oeuvre. One can see that it was painted with a great deal of pleasure. It dates from the happiest period of Van Gogh's life, when it really looked as if he could satisfy his 'need for gaiety and happiness, for hope and love'. Everyone recognizes this happiness, this optimism, in the *Sunflowers*, which explains the enormous demand for reproductions of it (66).

>66
Michael Wolf
Liu Yaoliang copying Van Gogh in Dafen, 2004

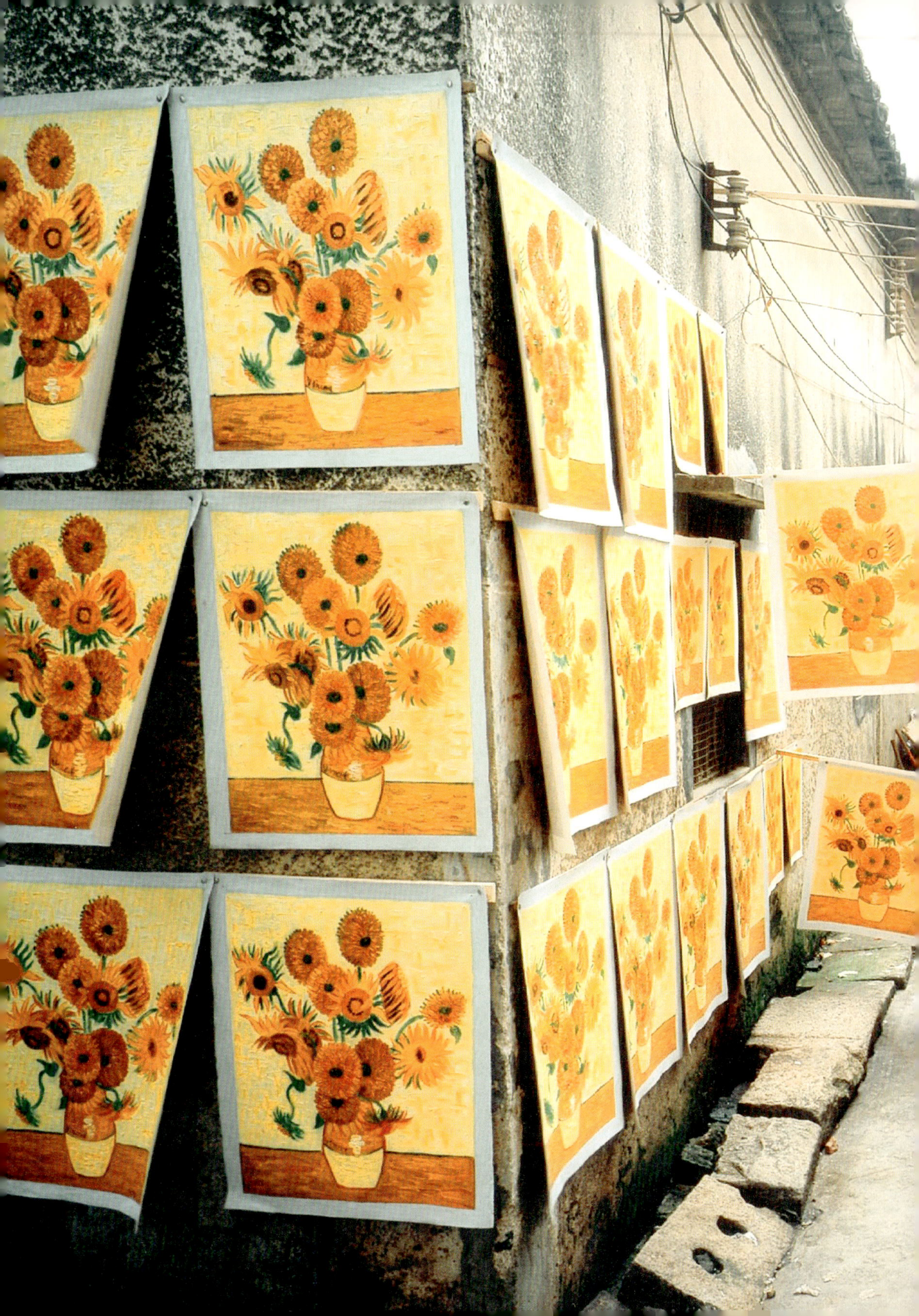

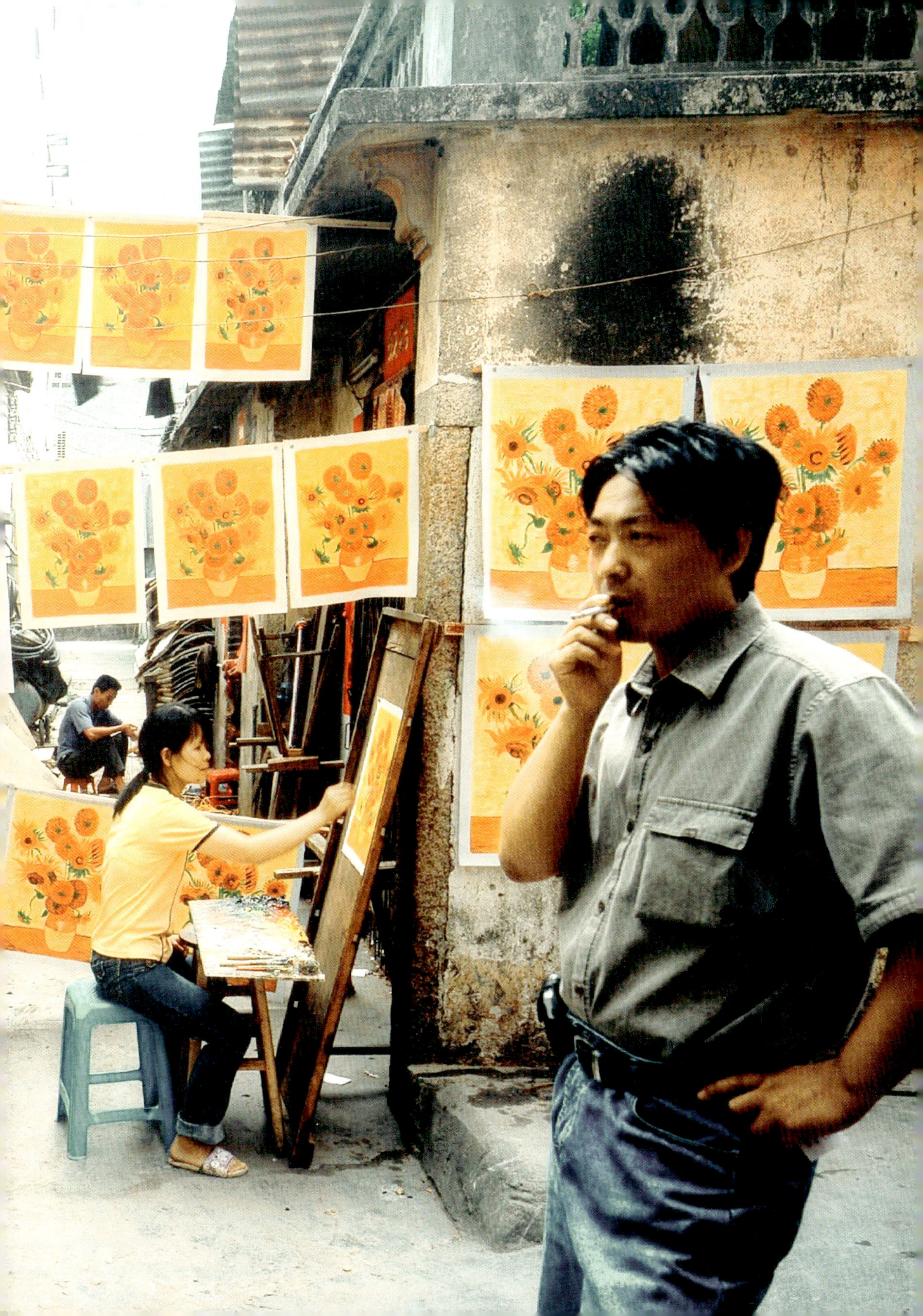

LITERATURE

Konrad Hoffmann, 'Zu Van Goghs Sonnenblumenbildern', *Zeitschrift für Kunstgeschichte*, 31 (1968), pp. 27–38

Roland Dorn, 'Van Gogh's Sunflowers series: *the fifth toile de 30*', *Van Gogh Museum Journal*, 1999, pp. 42–61

Debra N. Mancoff, *Sunflowers*, Chicago 2001

Douglas W. Druick and Peter Kort Zeegers, exhib. cat. *Van Gogh and Gauguin: the studio of the south*, Art Institute, Chicago, and Van Gogh Museum, Amsterdam, 2001

Louis van Tilborgh and Ella Hendriks, 'The Tokyo *Sunflowers*: a genuine repetition by Van Gogh or a Schuffenecker forgery?', *Van Gogh Museum Journal*, 2001, pp. 16–43

VAN GOGH'S CORRESPONDENCE

The quotations from Van Gogh's correspondence have been translated with some adaptation from *De brieven van Vincent van Gogh*, ed. H. Van Crimpen and M. Berens-Albert, 4 vols., The Hague 1990.

AUTHOR'S ACKNOWLEDGEMENTS

I would like to thank many colleagues from within and outside the museum for their kind assistance and advice. I am particularly grateful to Hans C.M. den Nijs, for without his botanical knowledge this book would have been very different. Thanks, too, go to Evert van Uitert and Chris Stolwijk for encouraging me to present a new interpretation of the *Sunflowers*. After completing his triptych with *La Berceuse* and *Sunflowers*, Van Gogh himself wrote that the still lifes of flowers symbolised 'gratitude' and with this in mind I dedicate this book to Truus van Tilborgh-Briedé.

VAN GOGH IN FOCUS

Van Gogh in focus is a series of books initiated by the Van Gogh Museum in Amsterdam on the life and work of Vincent van Gogh. Although so much has been written about this extraordinary artist, many questions still need to be answered or have been addressed only in specialist publications. These small, compact books examine the artist's oeuvre in different contexts throughout the various stages of his life. Each book focuses on unusual viewpoints in Van Gogh's art – such as his remarkable paintings of sunflowers, his passionate correspondence, or his deep love of nature – and presents many new facts and insights. The series is fully illustrated with documents as well as paintings and drawings by Van Gogh.

Already published in this series:
Peter Hecht, *Van Gogh and Rembrandt* (2006)
Louis van Tilborgh, *Van Gogh and Japan* (2006)
Leo Jansen, *Van Gogh and his letters* (2007)
Hans Luijten, *Van Gogh and love* (2007)

For recent information about new and upcoming titles:
www.vangoghmuseum.com/museumpublications

ILLUSTRATIONS

All works in the collection of the Van Gogh Museum reproduced in this book are the property of the Vincent van Gogh Foundation. All photographic rights are reserved by the institutions indicated in the captions and by the photographers:

Ill. 3: bequest of Charlotte Dorrance Wright, 1978
Ill. 6: photo RMN/© Hervé Lewandowski
Ill. 10: bpk/Nationalgalerie, SMB/Jörg P. Anders
Ill. 11: Ailsa Mellon Bruce Collection, courtesy of the Board of Trustees
Ill. 20: Rogers Fund, 1949
Ill. 23: bequest of John T. Spaulding
Ill. 26: H.O. Havemeyer Collection
Ill. 32: courtesy of Alhambra Antiques, Coral Gables (Fl.)
Ill. 33: courtesy of French Market Antiques, Fernandina Beach (Fl.), Jimmy Huston
Ill. 50: bequest of Walter H. and Leonore Annenberg, 2002
Ill 51: The Mr and Mrs Carrol S. Tyson, Jr. Collection
Ill. 60: courtesy Eykyn Maclean, LLC
Ill. 61: from: James Putnan, *Art and Artifact. The Museum as Medium*, London 2001, p.91
Ill. 65: © 2008 Gerhard Glück und Lappan Verlag, D-26121 Oldenburg
Ill. 66: © Laif/Hollandse Hoogte

Front cover: Vincent van Gogh, *Sunflowers* (detail), 1889, Van Gogh Museum, Amsterdam
Title page: Vincent van Gogh, *Sunflowers* (detail), 1887, Kröller-Müller Museum, Otterlo
Back cover: Vincent van Gogh, *Sunflowers* (detail), 1887, The Metropolitan Museum of Art, New York, Rogers Fund, 1949

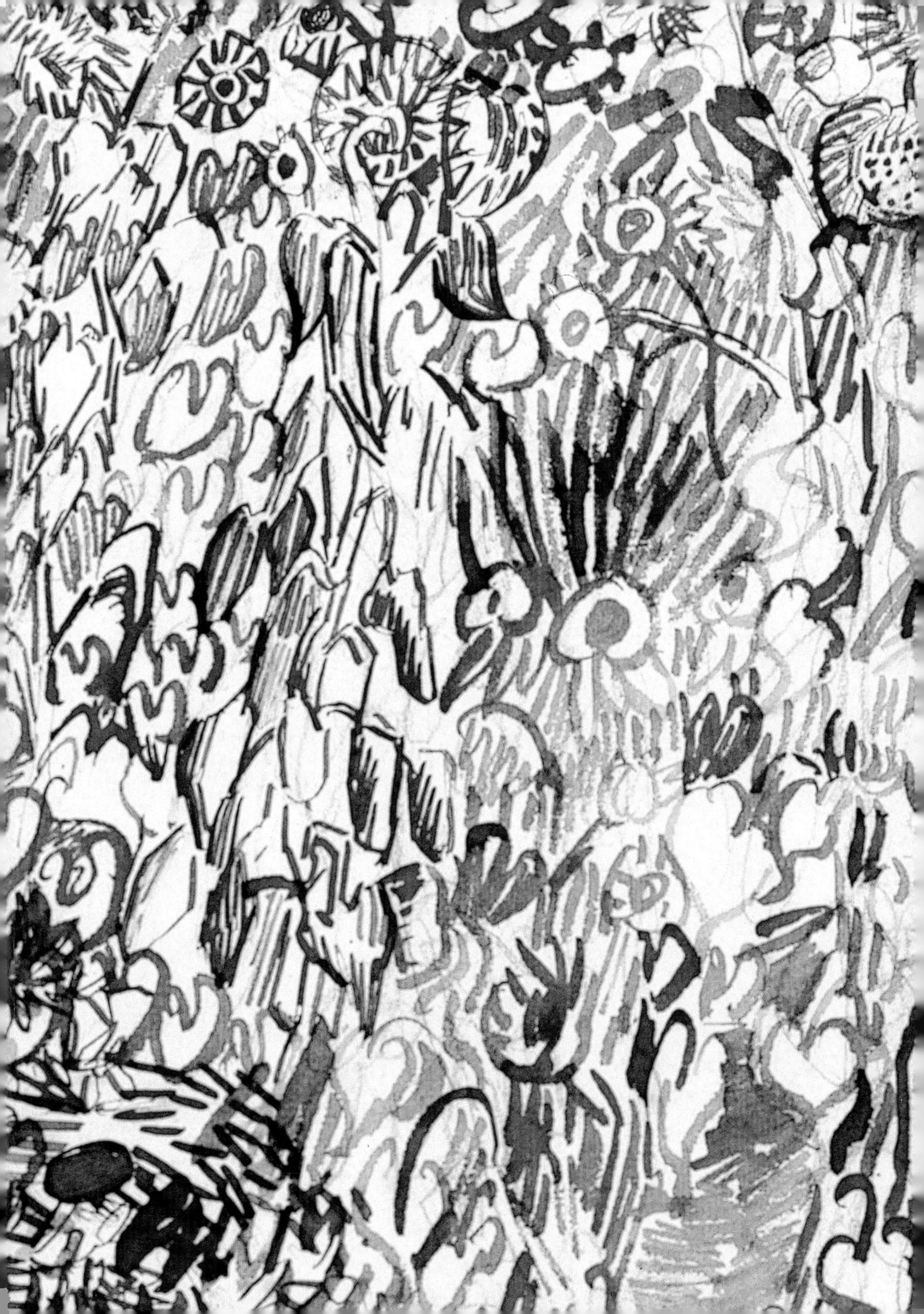

Van Gogh in focus is published under the auspices of the Van Gogh Museum, Amsterdam

Editorial board *Van Gogh in focus*
Chris Stolwijk, Leo Jansen, Heidi Vandamme, Suzanne Bogman

Head of publications
Suzanne Bogman

Editorial assistant
Geri Klazema

Photographic assistant
Fieke Pabst

Translation
Michael Hoyle

Text editing
Paul Holberton

Production
Tijdsbeeld & Pièce Montée, Ghent
Ronny Gobyn (director)

Coordination
Hannelore Duflou, Tijdsbeeld & Pièce Montée, Ghent

Graphic design and typesetting
Griet Van Haute, Ghent

Colour separation and printing
Die Keure, Bruges

© 2008 Van Gogh Museum, Amsterdam
www.vangoghmuseum.com
ISBN 978 907931 0050

No part of this book may be reproduced in any form, by print, photoprint,
microfilm or any other means without written permission from the publisher.